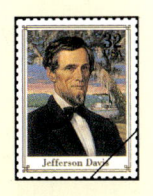

THE CIVIL WAR
1861 - 1865
A COLLECTION OF U.S. COMMEMORATIVE STAMPS

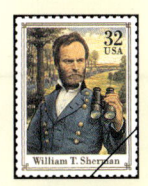

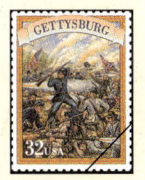

Contents

Introduction 4
Harriet Ross Tubman 6
Jefferson Finis Davis 10
Joseph Eggleston Johnston 14
Monitor versus Virginia 18
Thomas Johnathan Jackson 22
Shiloh 26
Winfield Scott Hancock 30
Clara Harlowe Barton 34
Robert Edward Lee 38
Chancellorsville 44
Frederick Douglass 48
Raphael Semmes 52
Gettysburg 56
Abraham Lincoln 62
Phoebe Yates Levy Pember 66
William Tecumseh Sherman 70
Stand Watie 74
David Glasgow Farragut 78
Mary Boykin Miller Chesnut 82
Ulysses S. Grant 86
The story behind the stamps 92

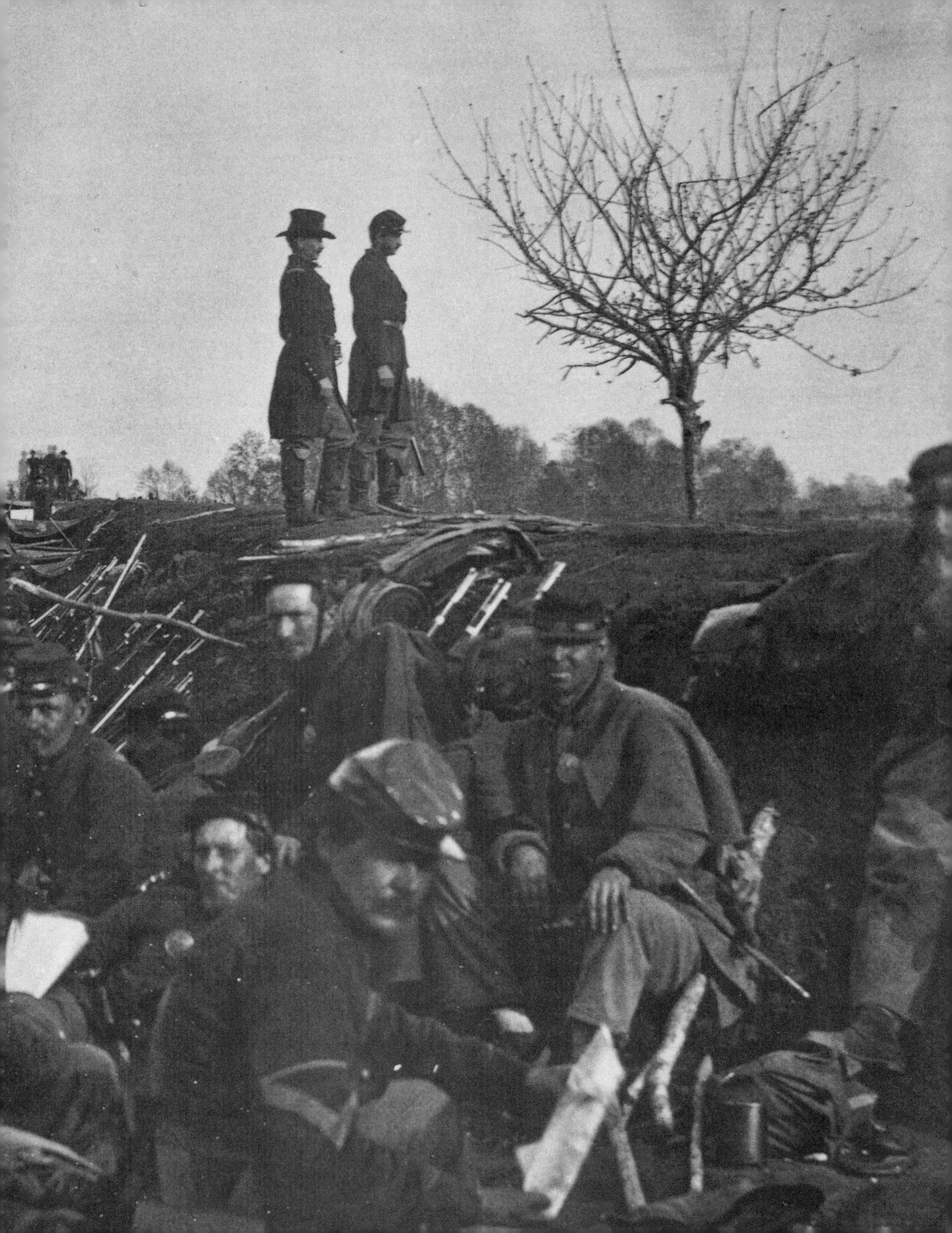

The Civil War

Even more than the American Revolution, the Civil War has defined our national character. The violence and valor, and the nobility of the combatants' cause, each fighting to preserve a "sacred" truth, are enshrined in the American consciousness.

The flow of time over the past 130 years, however, allows us to reexamine a softened image, to see the broad contours with a new clarity, and to feel its human side with keener poignancy. An example of this perspective is Ken Burns' Civil War documentary narrated, in part, through the words of the men and women who experienced the war. Their voices speak to us not as Northerners or Southerners, but as Americans caught in a tragic tumult.

It is fitting, then, that the U.S. Postal Service chose the Civil War as the subject of its second issue of "Classic Collection" stamps. This sheet of 20 stamps reflects the war through portraits of 16 very different individuals and four battles. Like the Classic Collection for "Legends of the West," each Civil War stamp has a short text on the back describing the event or identifying the person.

Naturally, there is no way to represent such an epic episode in history with 20 small images. But the people and battles that we have selected truly do epitomize the virtues that both sides adhered to—courage, duty and above all a shared conviction that right would prevail. Many of the men and women chosen to exemplify these values are enshrined in history and legend: Abraham Lincoln, Robert E. Lee, Jefferson Davis and Admiral Farragut. But these stamps honor others whose praises also deserve to be sung: Stand Watie, an American Indian and confederate general; diarist Mary Chesnut, a prescient chronicler of the war; abolitionist Harriet Tubman, who led 200 fellow blacks to freedom via the Underground Railroad; and "Angel of the Battlefield" Clara Barton, a fearless nurse at Antietam and battles in Virginia.

The choices for this series go far beyond "political correctness." In simplest terms, they are a reminder that this great war affected everyone: soldier and civilian, man and woman, black, white, and Native American. On a deeper level, each picture asks us to take a fresh look at cherished notions, to realize, for instance, that courage and bravery were not the exclusive property of generals.

Students of the Civil War will be disappointed at the omission of some who deserve to be commemorated. Besides Longstreet, Sheridan, Beauregard, Thomas, and a score of other generals there are other heroes and heroines who could not be included: Ely Parker, a brilliant Seneca Indian who was Grant's military secretary and who formally wrote out Grant's surrender terms for Lee at Appomattox; or Captain Sally Parker, the only woman commissioned by the CSA, who operated a Confederate hospital at her own expense.

Even so, these stamps are a stunning testament to the Civil War. Stunning because each one has been painstakingly executed from the most accurate pictorial sources and research available. Stunning, too, because they are exquisite little windows on history. As an historian, I am excited to think that these stamps may encourage people to learn more about individuals and events that have been an endless source of fascination and wonder to me and to countless others for so long.

James McPherson

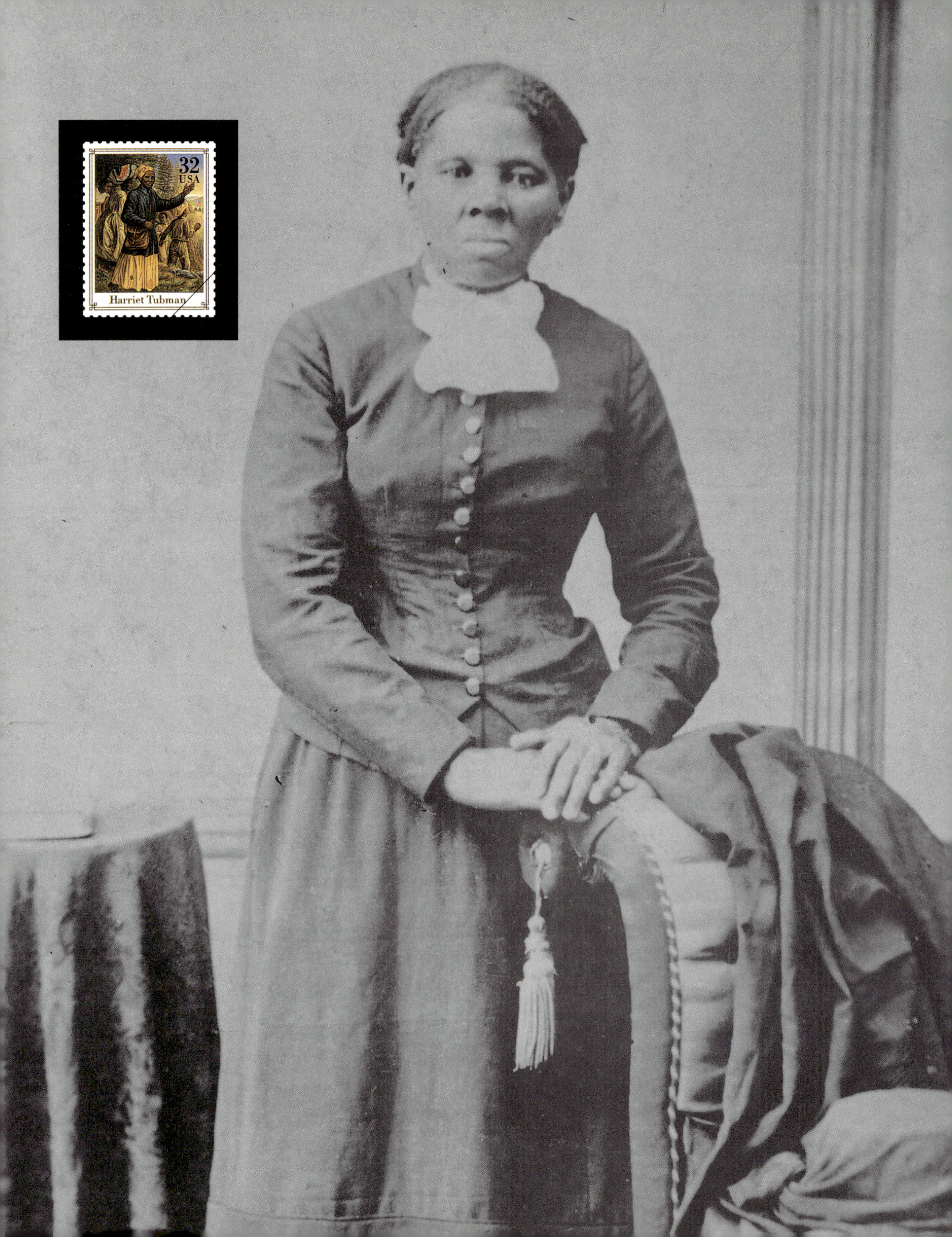
32
USA
Harriet Tubman

Harriet Ross Tubman
c. 1821-1913

Harriet Tubman's very person was a mute catalogue of slavery's commonplace brutalities. Her spare, wiry frame reflected an underfed childhood and the relentless, backbreaking labor that was her lot as a field hand. Her guarded countenance and reticent manner bespoke a life in which any spontaneous word or action might elicit a swift kick or a vicious whipping. The bandana she tied low on her brow concealed a disfiguring scar, the result of a near-fatal blow to the head by an enraged overseer; all her life, she suffered recurring seizures, racking headaches and spells of sudden unconsciousness.

Tubman escaped slavery in 1849, in her late twenties, when she fled her master's Maryland plantation and made her way to Pennsylvania. Once free, she joined the Underground Railway, the secret network of safehouses and sympathetic people that helped spirit as many as 100,000 blacks out of the South between 1830 and 1860. Over the following decade, Tubman herself accounted for more than 200 escapes, risking her life and her own hard-won freedom as the Railway's most courageous and successful "conductor." Sometimes disguised as a man, other times posing as a frail old woman, she made at least 15 covert forays into the South to escort groups of slaves to freedom. As she proudly related to her biographer years later, "I never ran my train off the track and I never lost a passenger."

The devoutly religious Tubman displayed courage that earned her near-mythic status among abolitionists, one of whom called her in 1859 "the greatest heroine of the age." In slave quarters throughout the South, where her exploits were related in awed whispers, she was known as "Moses". Plantation owners put a $40,000 price on her head. Like other abolitionists, Harriet Tubman saw the Civil War as a moral crusade against slavery, and she joined in with characteristic grit, serving as a volunteer cook, laundress, nurse and sometimes spy for Union forces, using the talents she had honed in the Railway on scouting expeditions. In postwar years, she worked tirelessly with black churches and women's organizations to raise funds for freed slaves and set up schools for their children. At her death in 1913, in an Auburn, New York, home she had established for needy blacks, she was buried with full military honors. ♣

Tokens of the slave system that Harriet Tubman (*opposite*) campaigned against, metal tags such as this one, identifying its wearer by number and listing his occupation as porter, had to be worn by all slaves in Charleston, South Carolina. After 1848, free blacks there were required to wear the tags as well.

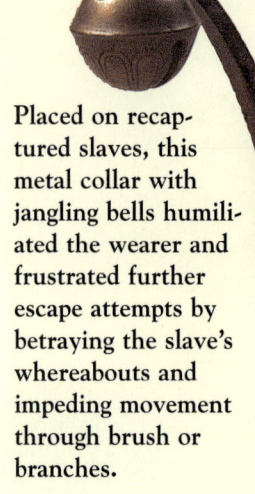

Placed on recaptured slaves, this metal collar with jangling bells humiliated the wearer and frustrated further escape attempts by betraying the slave's whereabouts and impeding movement through brush or branches.

From 1858 to 1861, this slave-trading house in Alexandria, Virginia, held men, women and children in guarded rooms while whites looked them over for purchase.

Pictured here with her rifle, Underground Railroad conductor Harriet Tubman carried a gun to fend off slave-catchers—and remind reluctant escapees that there was no turning back.

$100 REWARD!

RANAWAY

From the undersigned, living on Current River, about twelve miles above Doniphan, in Ripley County, Mo., on 2nd of March, 1860, A NEGRO MAN, about 30 years old, weighs about 160 pounds; high forehead, with a scar on it; had on brown pants and coat very much worn, and an old black wool hat; shoes size No. 11.

The above reward will be given to any person who may apprehend this said negro out of the State; and fifty dollars if apprehended in this State outside of Ripley county, or $25 if taken in Ripley county.

APOS TUCKER.

A poster offers a reward for an unnamed fugitive from Missouri. The full $100 applied if the slave was caught out of state.

During the war, Tubman helped fugitives from the Confederacy find work like this group, shown washing clothes for Union soldiers.

The light from this hitching post marked a safe house for escaped slaves in New Hope, Pennsylvania.

Pictured above after the war, Tubman cherished memories of trips she made in the 1850s to bring to freedom members of her own family *(left)*.

✯✯✯✯✯✯✯✯✯✯
CIVIL WAR TIME LINE
✯✯✯✯✯✯✯✯✯✯

1860

November 6 - Lincoln elected president.

December 20 - South Carolina secedes.

December 26 - Federal garrison transfers to Fort Sumter.

1861

January 9 - *Star of the West* is fired upon. Mississippi secedes.

January 10 - Florida secedes.

January 11 - Alabama secedes.

January 19 - Georgia secedes.

January 26 - Louisiana secedes.

February 1 - Texas secedes.

February 4 - Convention of seceded states meets in Montgomery, Alabama.

February 8 - Confederate Constitution adopted.

February 9 - Jefferson Davis elected provisional president of the Confederate States; Alexander Stephens named vice-president.

February 18 - Davis inaugurated president of the Confederacy.

March 4 - Abraham Lincoln inaugurated president of the United States.

April 11 - Confederates demand surrender of Fort Sumter.

April 12 - Fort Sumter fired upon.

Jefferson Davis

JEFFERSON FINIS DAVIS
1808-1889

Proud, touchy, loyal, rash, fearless, vain, hot-tempered, generous, imperious, deluded. These were the qualities manifest in Confederate president Jefferson Davis, a complex and tormented man whose mix of flaws and virtues seemed at times to embody the South he led in its years of deepest crisis.

Kentucky-born, and raised on a modest Mississippi plantation in what was then a virtual wilderness, Davis was a sensitive and imaginative boy. In 1824, he entered West Point, leaving four years later with a passion for all things military and a deep thirst for fame on the battlefield. But his seven-year army career, spent in remote frontier outposts, was undistinguished. It ended in 1835 with his return to Mississippi and 10 melancholy years as a planter and near-recluse following the death of his first wife. His second marriage, in 1845, to the daughter of a socially prominent family, and his service in the Mexican War the following year, brought him out of his shell and into a career in politics. A staunch proponent of slavery, Davis served as a United States congressman, senator and secretary of war. He was in the Senate when Mississippi left the Union in January 1861.

Less than a month later, a convention of all the seceding states named him president of the new Confederacy—a compromise choice whose elevation to chief executive fully pleased no one, least of all himself. When notified by telegram of his appointment, he looked so stricken that his wife thought some catastrophe had befallen the family. Davis had hoped to win glory as commander of the Southern armies. As president he faced a far more daunting task.

The South lacked the resources to sustain large-scale military operations. And Davis' own inflated view of himself as a strategist led to constant meddling with his generals. Moreover, the contentiously independent Confederate states resisted central authority, and the president's efforts to control unruly political factions made him reviled as a would-be despot.

Seemingly incapable of compromise, Davis was so persistently at battle with his civilian and military foes that it rendered him, wrote his wife, "a mere mass of throbbing nerves." He remained loyal to the Confederate cause well after it was clearly lost, urging Southerners to fight on even as he fled the Union troops that occupied Richmond on April 3, 1865, just days before Lee's surrender at Appomattox. He was captured by Federal cavalry on May 10. A warm shawl wrapped around his shoulders against an unseasonable chill led to the wounding legend that he had tried to escape disguised in his wife's hoop skirt. Accused of treason, Davis was imprisoned for two years. He lived his remaining 22 years in poverty, failing at a succession of business ventures and writing his memoirs. ♣

Confederate national flags were flown over military fortifications or public buildings such as the capitol at Richmond. President Jefferson Davis *(opposite)* was both revered and scorned by Southerners.

The executive mansion in Richmond was photographed on April 12, 1865, nine days after Davis fled the Federals. The Great Seal of the Confederacy *(inset)* bears the martial figure of George Washington and a Latin motto that reads: "With God as defender." The envelope bearing a Davis stamp *(inset)* was made of wallpaper for lack of stationery.

Varina Howell Davis remained in Richmond with her husband and four children *(left)* until the last days of the Confederacy. The couple lost their first child in infancy; another boy, four-year-old Joseph, died in a balcony fall in April 1864.

This portrait of Jefferson Davis, the only one painted from life during the Civil War, depicts the Confederate president at the age of 55. An associate called the enigmatic Davis "the Sphinx of the Confederacy."

$360,000 REWARD!

THE PRESIDENT OF THE UNITED STATES

Has issued his Proclamation, announcing that the Bureau of Military Justice has reported upon indubitable evidence that

JEFFERSON DAVIS, CLEMENT CLAY, JACOB THOMPSON, GEO. N. SAUNDERS, BEVERLY TUCKER, and WM. C. CLEARY,

incited and concerted the assassination of Mr. Lincoln, and the attack upon Mr. Seward.

He therefore, offers for the arrest of Davis, Clay and Thompson $100,000 each; for that of Saunders and Tucker $25,000 each, for that of Cleary $10,000.

May 9, 1865.   JAM...
                  Major Gen. Uni...

The broadside above announces rewards offered for the capture of Jefferson Davis and five other Confederate leaders. At right, the ambulance carrying Davis into captivity arrives at army headquarters in Macon, Georgia, on May 13, 1865.

At peace at last, Davis sits on a veranda of an old friend's Mississippi estate. There he wrote *The Rise and Fall of the Confederate Government*, which was published in 1881, eight years before he died.

★★★★★★★★★★★
1861
★★★★★★★★★★★

April 13 - Fort Sumter surrenders.

April 14 - Federal garrison marches out of Fort Sumter.

April 17 - Virginia convention votes for secession.

April 19 - Riots in Baltimore, Maryland. Lincoln declares blockade of the Confederate ports.

April 20 - Federals evacuate Gosport Navy Yard in Norfolk, Virginia. Robert E. Lee confirmed as commander of Virginia forces.

April 27 - Lincoln suspends privilege of writ of habeus corpus.

April 29 - Maryland house of delegates votes against secession.

May 6 - Arkansas and Tennessee pass secession ordinances. Confederate States recognize a state of war with the United States.

May 10 - Riots in Saint Louis, Missouri.

May 13 - Federal troops occupy Baltimore, Maryland.

May 20 - North Carolina secedes.

May 23 - Virginia citizens ratify secession ordinance.

May 24 - Federal troops occupy Alexandria, Virginia.

June 3 - Skirmish at Philippi, Virginia.

June 10 - Engagement at Big Bethel, Virginia.

13

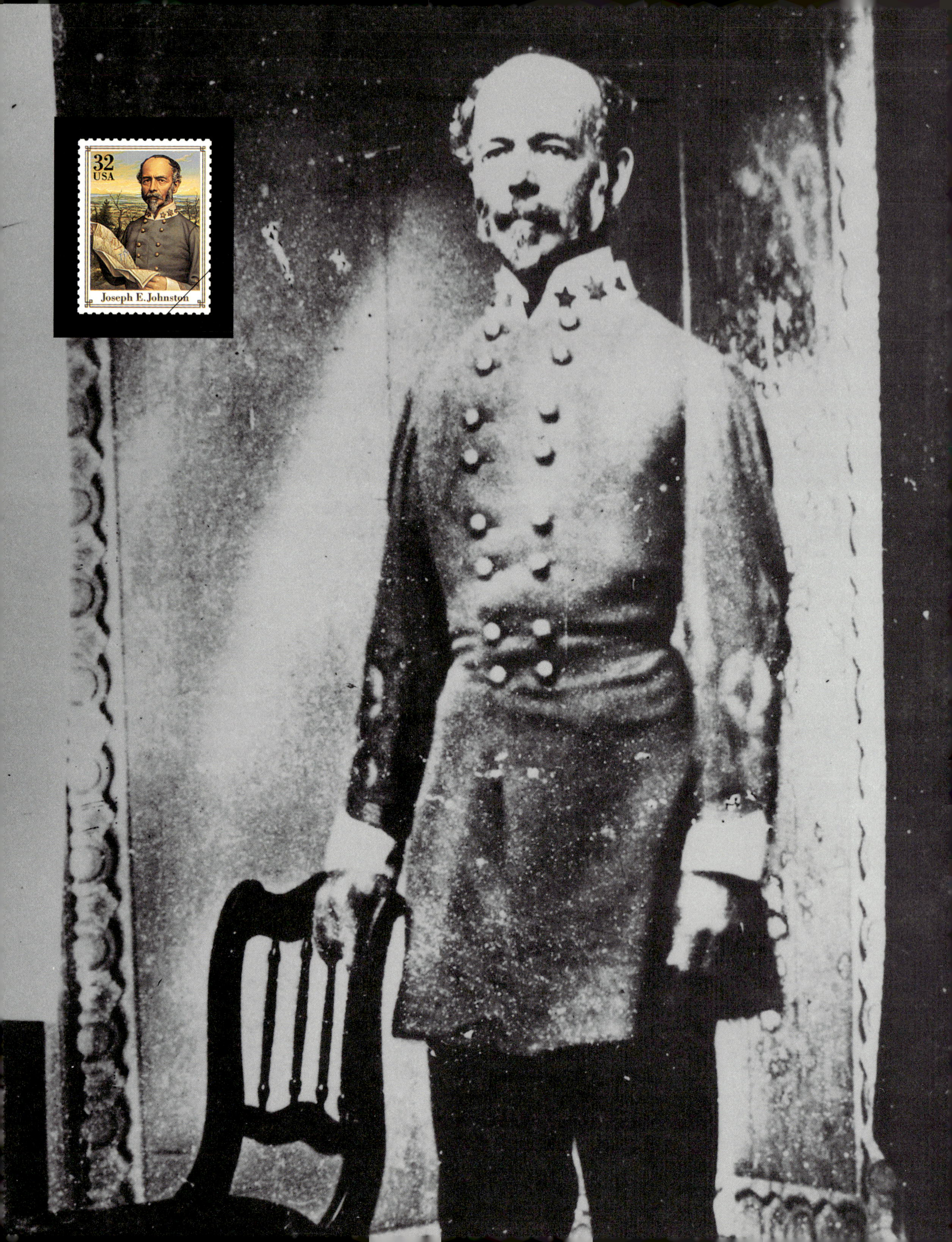
32
USA
Joseph E. Johnston

JOSEPH EGGLESTON JOHNSTON
1807-1891

When a Yankee shell fragment at the Battle of Seven Pines knocked Joseph E. Johnston out of action in May of 1862, many anxious Southerners feared that the Confederate cause had been dealt an irreparable blow. Johnston was a genuine Confederate hero, and one of the South's finest officers. A Mexican War veteran, he was serving as quartermaster general of the U.S. Army when he resigned his commission in April 1861 to serve his native Virginia—one of the highest ranking army officers to cast his lot with the Confederacy. Commanding troops at Harpers Ferry in July 1861, he hurried them to Manassas in time to repulse the Federals at Bull Run and claim victory in the war's first engagement. In the winter of 1862, realizing that his Army of Northern Virginia might soon be outflanked at Manassas, he skillfully executed a series of tactical withdrawals that blocked General George McClellan's drive on Richmond. But in doing so Johnston drew the ire of Confederate president Jefferson Davis, who expected his general to attack, not retreat. Finally, on May 31, with the Federals just 12 miles from Richmond, Johnston launched a counterthrust at Seven Pines. When he fell wounded, Robert E. Lee took command of the army.

Johnston remained a hero to his men, who prized his devotion to their welfare. Privately, Davis may have agreed with the hunting companion of Johnston who contended that in stalking game as in waging war, the general was too fussy, "too much afraid to miss and risk his fine reputation." But such was his stature that Davis continued to rely on him. In late 1863, Johnston took charge of the battered Army of Tennessee and sought to keep William T. Sherman from descending on Atlanta. Johnston rehabilitated the army and responded so alertly to Federal flanking moves that Sherman marveled at his "lynx-eyed watchfulness." But time and again, Johnston was forced to give ground. In July 1864, an exasperated Davis removed him in favor of John Bell Hood, whose costly attacks failed to save Atlanta.

In February 1865, Johnston resumed command of what remained of the Army of Tennessee. Unwilling to expend lives without hope of victory, he rejected Davis' suggestion that the struggle be prolonged. "Our people are tired of war," he insisted, "feel themselves whipped, and will not fight." The breach between Davis and Johnston never healed, but the general reconciled with his former adversary Sherman, to whom he surrendered. After representing Virginia in Congress in postwar days, Johnston honored Sherman by marching through the rain in his funeral procession—then took to bed with pneumonia and died. ♣

Confederate general Joseph Johnston's sword was first used by his father against the British during the Revolutionary War. When Johnston fell wounded at Seven Pines in 1862, he refused to leave the field until the weapon was retrieved.

"He was loved, respected, admired; yea almost worshipped by his troops."

*Private. Sam Watkins,
1st Tennessee Infantry, C.S.A.*

With arm raised, General Johnston rallies a Georgia regiment at Manassas on July 21, 1861. Johnston, portrayed at top in 1855, repulsed the Federals at Manassas by hurrying reinforcements to the front with simple orders: "Go where the fire is hottest."

Johnston's field telescope

16

This silk battle flag was sewn for General Johnston by a group of patriotic women in Richmond.

Former classmates at West Point, Joseph Johnston and Robert E. Lee *(right)* were both 63 when they met again in Savannah in April 1870, five years after surrendering the Confederacy's two largest armies. A reporter there noted on Lee's face a look of "inexpressible sadness." Lee died that same year, while Johnston—pictured at left shortly after the war—lived on for more than two decades.

★★★★★★★★★★★★
1 8 6 1
★★★★★★★★★★★★

June 17 - Engagement at Boonville, Missouri.

June 19 - Pro-Union convention sets up "provisional government" of Virginia at Wheeling. Francis Pierpoint named "provisional governor".

July 4 - Lincoln calls special session of Congress to pass war measures.

July 5 - Engagement at Carthage, Missouri.

July 11 - Engagement at Rich Mountain, Virginia.

July 18 - Engagement at Blackburn's Ford, Virginia.

July 21 - Battle of Bull Run (First Manassas).

July 26 - Federals surrender Fort Fillmore in New Mexico Territory.

July 31 - Ulysses S. Grant appointed brigadier general.

August 10 - Battle of Wilson's Creek, Missouri.

August 28 - Capture of Fort Hatteras, North Carolina.

August 30 - Federal General John C. Fremont issues local emancipation proclamation in Missouri.

September 6 - Federal gunboats capture Paducah, Kentucky.

September 11-16 Cheat Mountain campaign, western Virginia.

September 12 - Siege of Lexington, Missouri, begins.

17

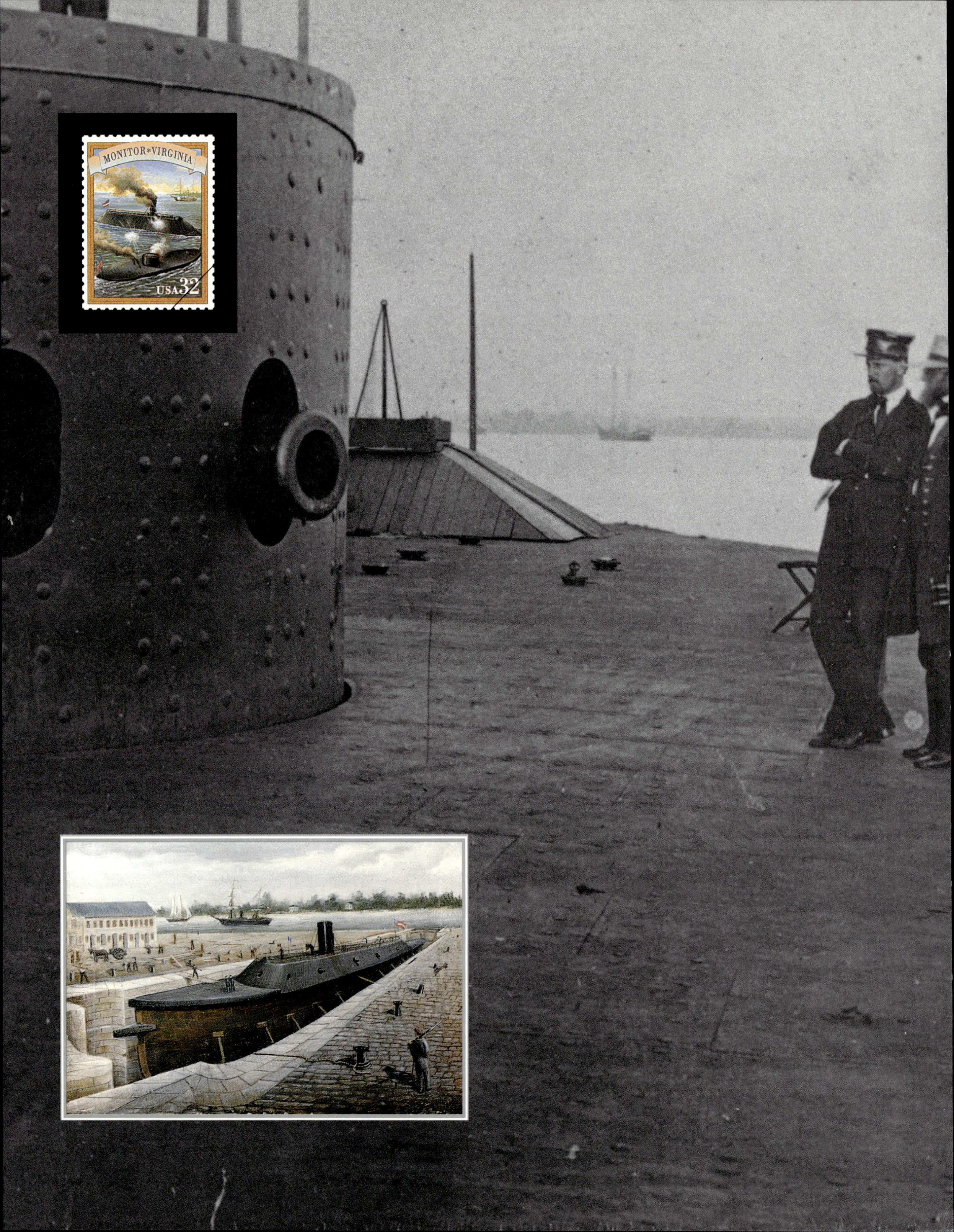
MONITOR ✶ VIRGINIA
USA 32

MONITOR VERSUS VIRGINIA
MARCH 9, 1862

On March 8, 1862, a gunboat enforcing the Union blockade of Hampton Roads—a strategic channel at the mouth of Virginia's James River—was approached by a strange vessel that looked to the boat's skipper like "the roof of a very big barn belching smoke as from a chimney on fire." This behemoth was the pioneering Confederate ironclad *Virginia*, known to Yankees as the *Merrimack* for the scuttled Federal steam-driven warship from which it had been converted. Intent on busting the blockade, Confederates had salvaged the wreck and constructed a new deck, equipped with 10 big guns and sheathed in four inches of iron. Jutting from its prow like a spearhead was a hull-puncturing iron ram.

The *Virginia* wreaked havoc. Brushing aside the pesky Union gunboat—whose shots glanced harmlessly off the sloping casemate that wily Confederates had greased with pork fat—the ironclad rammed the 24-gun sloop *Cumberland* and sank it. Then the *Virginia* turned on the frigate *Congress* and set it ablaze with shellfire. News of the debacle led Lincoln's secretary of war, Edwin Stanton, to alert ports all along the coast: "Man your guns. Block your harbors. The *Merrimac* is coming."

Yet the navy responded with firepower of its own. Late on March 8, the Union's novel ironclad, the *Monitor*, sailed into Hampton Roads, prepared to do battle. Unlike the *Virginia*, this vessel was conceived as an ironclad. Although it carried only two guns, they revolved neatly on a turret, and the ship's low profile offered only a small target. Furthermore, the flat-bottomed *Monitor* could creep through waters as shallow as 11 feet, while the *Virginia* required twice that depth.

The showdown came early on March 9. For four hours, the two ironclads exchanged fierce fire, to little effect. Running short of ammunition, the *Virginia*'s skipper, Lieutenant Catesby Jones, tried in vain to ram his nimble foe and ended up trading shots with the *Monitor* from point-blank range. Jones' counterpart, Lieutenant John Worden, was disabled when a shell from the *Virginia* exploded against the viewing slit of his pilot house, but the *Monitor* then drifted into water too shallow for the *Virginia* to follow, and the epic duel ended in a draw. Afterward, the *Virginia* put in for lengthy repairs, and in May Confederates abandoned the shipyard where it was docked and destroyed the vessel to keep it out of enemy hands. The *Monitor* came to grief as well, sinking in a storm off Cape Hatteras that December. The potential of ironclads had been forcefully demonstrated, however, and the two sides would turn out dozens more before the war was through. ♣

This playing card from a set produced after the duel depicts the *Virginia* (left); the ship was converted at a yard near Norfolk (opposite, inset).

Another card from the same set depicts the *Monitor* (right), built in Brooklyn and unlike anything sailors had ever set foot on (opposite, background).

The *Monitor*—shielding the frigate *Minnesota* at right—duels with the *Virginia* at close range on March 9, 1862. The commanding officers of the two ironclads are shown at left in descending order: *Virginia*'s skipper, Franklin Buchanan, had been wounded the day before and was replaced by Catesby Jones. The *Monitor*'s captain, John Worden, was disabled in the battle on March 9 and turned over command to S. Dana Greene *(bottom)*.

Crewmen of the *Monitor* relax aboard the ironclad after the battle.

This northern postal cover served to commemorate the 1862 duel.

The *Virginia* carried this early seven-star Confederate ensign and an updated 11-star version, flown during the battle with the *Monitor*. The *Monitor* flew a U.S. ensign with 34 stars *(below)*, one for each state in the Union that the Federals were fighting to reconstruct.

1861

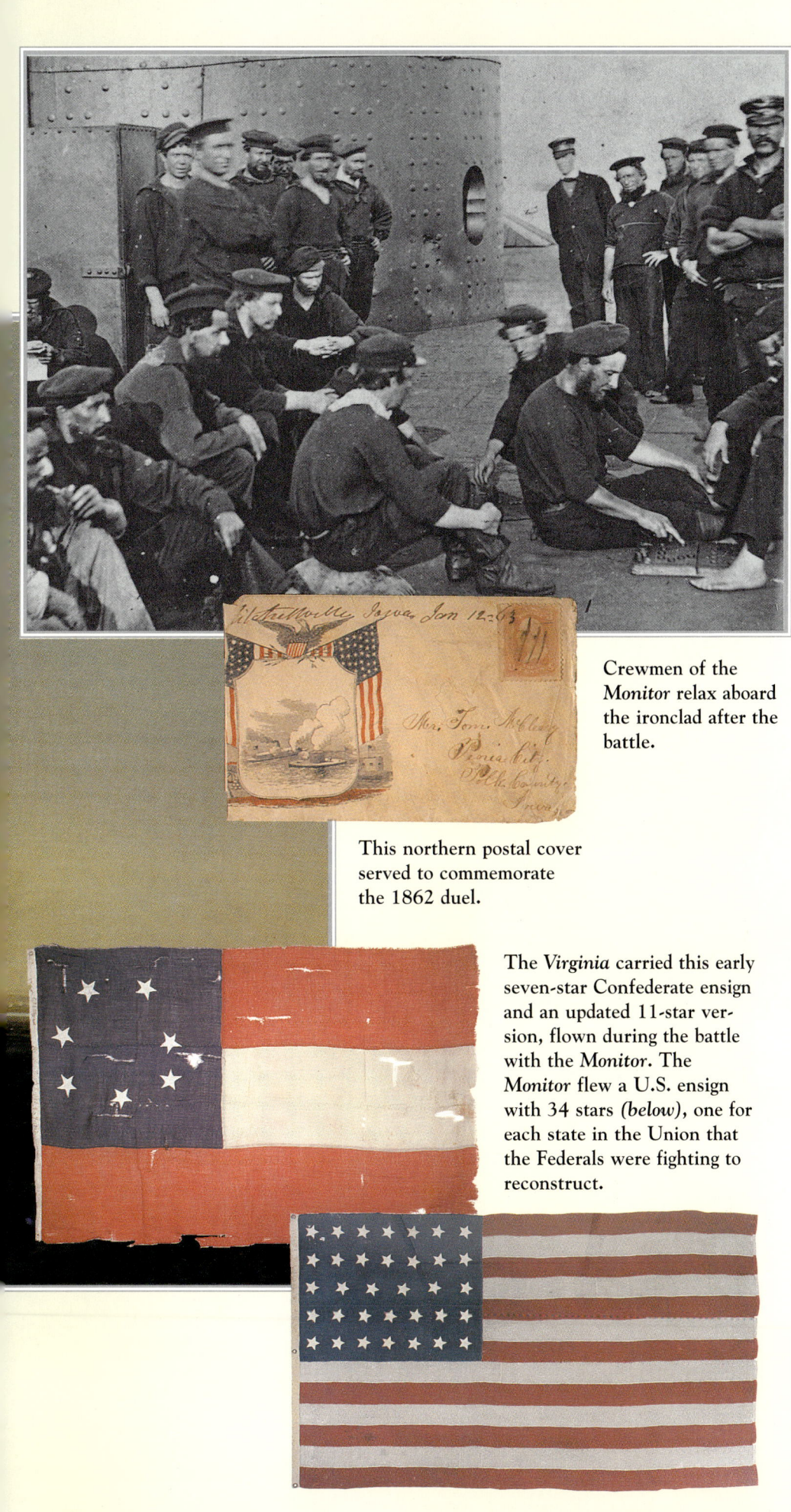

September 20 - Surrender of Lexington, Missouri.

October 21 - Battle of Ball's Bluff, Virginia.

October 24 - Transcontinental Telegraph completed.

November 1 - George B. McClellan appointed general-in-chief.

November 7 - Battle of Port Royal Sound, South Carolina. Engagement at Belmont, Missouri.

November 8 - Confederate envoys Mason and Slidell seized by U.S. Navy from British steamer *Trent*.

December 1 - United States Congress creates the Joint Committee on the Conduct of the War.

December 26 - United States releases Mason and Slidell.

1862

January 19 - Battle of Mill Springs (Logan's Cross Roads), Kentucky.

February 6 - Surrender of Fort Henry, Tennessee.

February 8 - Battle of Roanoke Island, North Carolina.

February 13 - Federal attack on Fort Donelson, Tennessee.

February 14 - Federal gunboats attack Fort Donelson, Tennessee.

February 16 - Surrender of Fort Donelson, Tennessee.

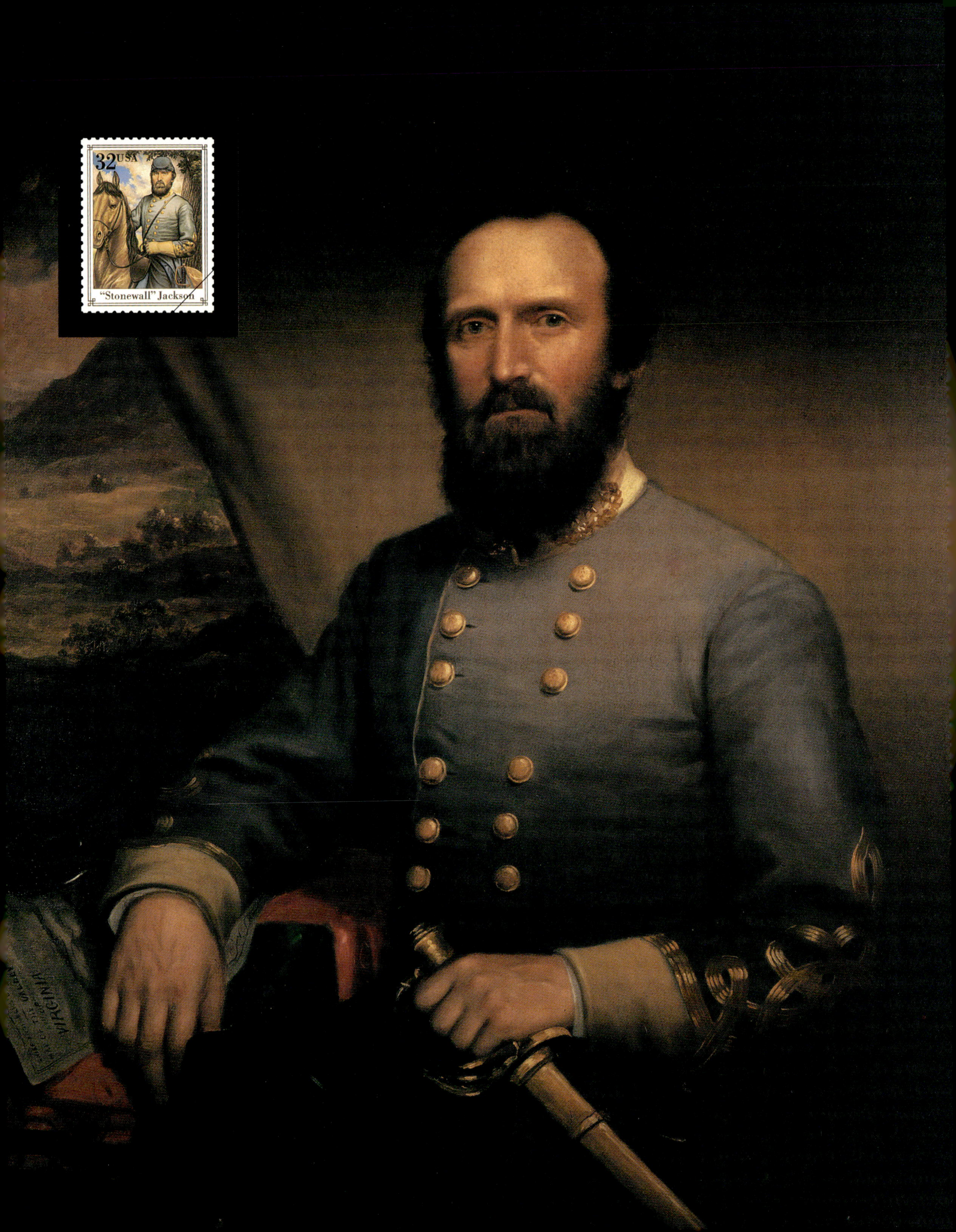
32 USA
"Stonewall" Jackson
VIRGINIA

Thomas Johnathan Jackson
1824-1863

On July 21, 1861, the South was losing the first great battle of the Civil War near the banks of Bull Run. Desperately trying to halt his retreating soldiers, Confederate general Barnard E. Bee spotted one Southern brigade that wasn't running. "There stands Jackson like a stone wall!" Bee shouted. "Rally behind the Virginians!" The new line held, and by day's end the Yankees had been routed from the field. General Thomas Jonathan Jackson, the man who had turned defeat into victory, would ever after be known as "Stonewall" Jackson.

Despite Jackson's West Point education and gallant service in the Mexican War, few of his contemporaries in 1861 imagined that the 37-year-old Virginia Military Institute professor would rise to the heights of military genius. Stern, quiet and deeply religious, Jackson was a true eccentric. He was stoop-shouldered and wore his cap pulled low over his piercing blue eyes. His uniform was rumpled and worn, his sword rusted in its scabbard. Jackson rarely shared his plans with his subordinates, and when he did speak his voice was so low and muffled that he was often unintelligible. A faithful churchgoer, he usually fell asleep during the sermon. He craved buttermilk to settle his chronic indigestion, yet snacked on lemons and raw onions. It was said that his habit of raising his left arm above his head stemmed from his belief that one side of his body was heavier than the other.

Yet Jackson possessed an iron will and a fervent devotion to the Southern cause. As one general put it, "praying and fighting appeared to be his idea of the whole duty of man." In Virginia's Shenandoah Valley in the spring of 1862, he confirmed his strategic brilliance. Though outnumbered four to one, Jackson defeated three Federal armies sent to trap his. Stonewall pushed his men hard; they marched so far and so fast that they were dubbed "Jackson's foot cavalry." His troops seemed to love him for it—they called him "Old Jack." A Yankee prisoner once grumbled, "Stonewall Jackson's men will follow him to the devil and he knows it."

In the battles of Second Manassas, Antietam and Fredericksburg, Jackson proved to be General Robert E. Lee's most trusted commander. At Chancellorsville, during May of 1863, Jackson's daring flank attack brought the Confederacy one of its greatest victories. But it was Stonewall's last fight. Riding forward in the dark, he was mistakenly shot by his own men. He died eight days later, after uttering these last words: "Let us cross over the river and rest under the shade of the trees." ♣

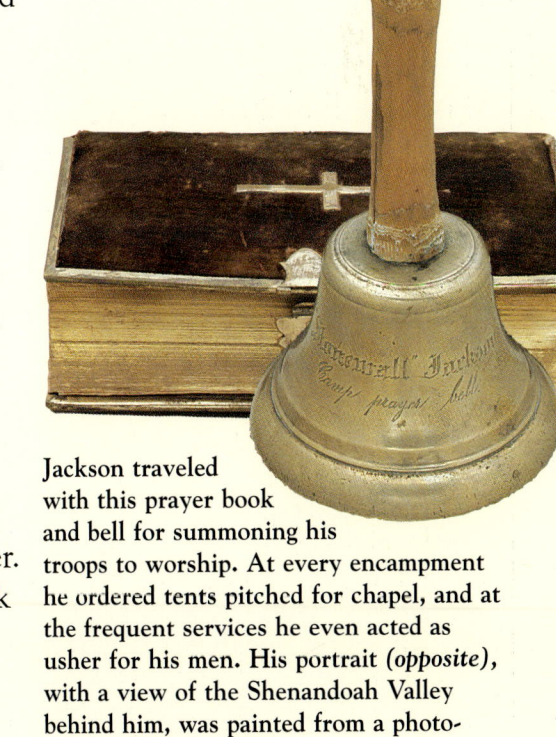

Jackson traveled with this prayer book and bell for summoning his troops to worship. At every encampment he ordered tents pitched for chapel, and at the frequent services he even acted as usher for his men. His portrait (*opposite*), with a view of the Shenandoah Valley behind him, was painted from a photograph taken in 1862.

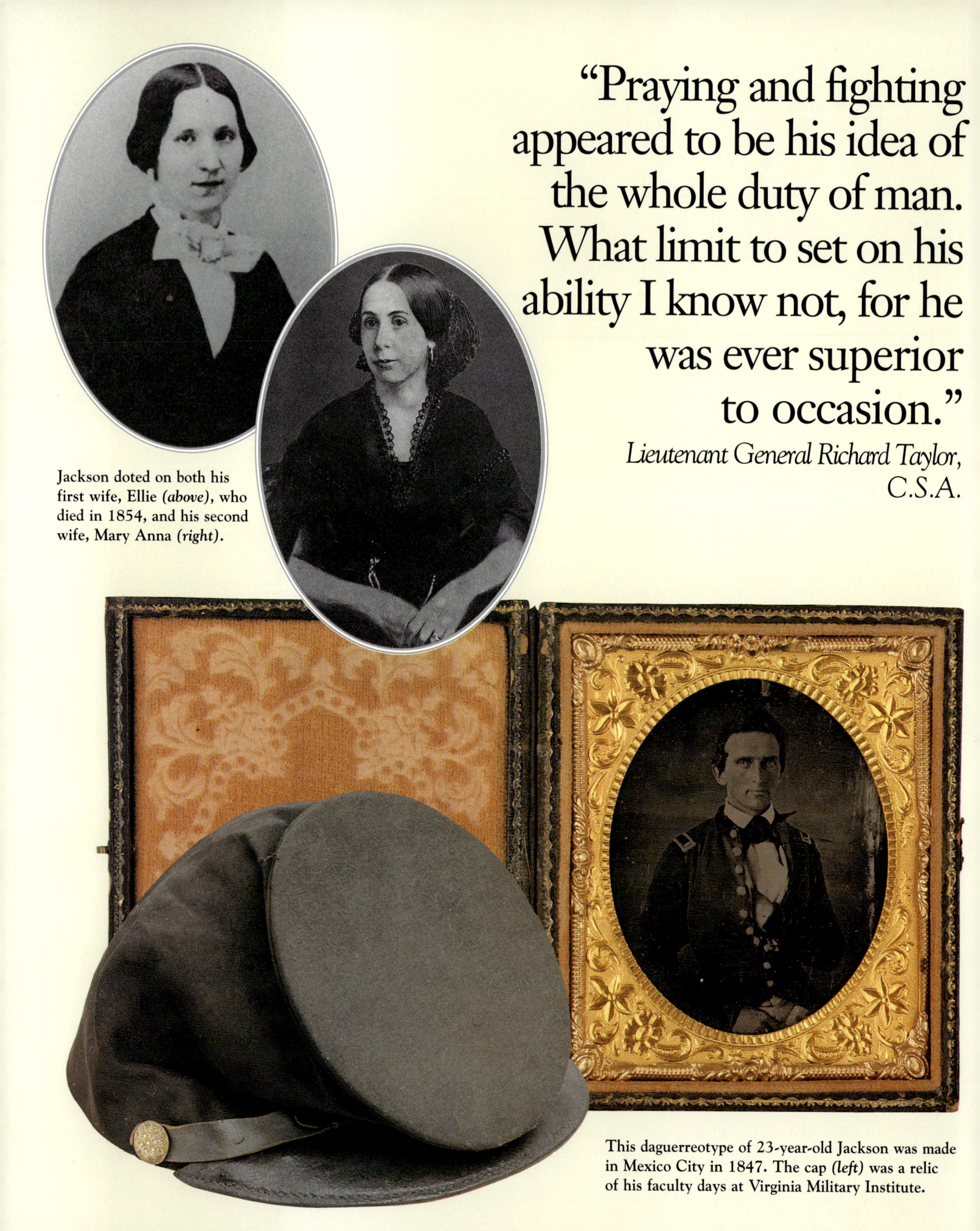

Jackson doted on both his first wife, Ellie *(above)*, who died in 1854, and his second wife, Mary Anna *(right)*.

"Praying and fighting appeared to be his idea of the whole duty of man. What limit to set on his ability I know not, for he was ever superior to occasion."

Lieutenant General Richard Taylor, C.S.A.

This daguerreotype of 23-year-old Jackson was made in Mexico City in 1847. The cap *(left)* was a relic of his faculty days at Virginia Military Institute.

24

Jackson sat for this photograph at his headquarters a few days before the fighting began at Chancellorsville. "I arranged his hair myself," his wife Mary Anna later wrote. "I never saw him look so handsome and noble." It was his last photograph.

The Confederate $500 bill bore Jackson's likeness.

Footsore and weary, Stonewall Jackson's troops nevertheless raise a cheer as they march past their commander on a spring day in the Shenandoah Valley in 1862.

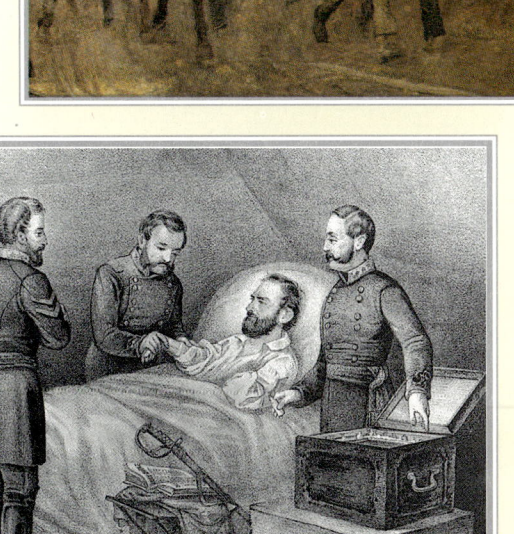

This engraving shows Stonewall Jackson succumbing to his wound in a tent rather than in the small house near Guinea Station where he actually died. His death was the "heartbreak of the Southern Confederacy," one of his officers wrote.

★★★★★★★★★★★★
1862
★★★★★★★★★★★★

February 21 - Engagement at Valverde, New Mexico Territory.

February 25 - Federal troops occupy Nashville, Tennessee.

March 6-8 Battle of Pea Ridge (Elkhorn Tavern), Arkansas.

March 8 - C.S.S. *Virginia* destroys Federal warships *Congress* and *Cumberland*.

March 9 - Battle between C.S.S. *Virginia* and U.S.S. *Monitor*.

March 14 - Federals capture New Madrid, Missouri, and New Bern, North Carolina.

March 23 - Battle of Kernstown, Virginia.

March 26 - Engagement at Apache Canyon, New Mexico Territory.

March 28 - Battle of Glorietta Pass, New Mexico Territory.

April 5 - Siege of Yorktown, Virginia, begins.

April 6-7 Battle of Shiloh (Pittsburg Landing), Tennessee. Capture of Island Number 10, Tennessee.

April 11 - Capture of Fort Pulaski, Georgia.

April 12 - The Great Locomotive Chase (Andrews Raid), Georgia.

April 18 - Federal fleet bombards Forts Jackson and St. Philip below New Orleans.

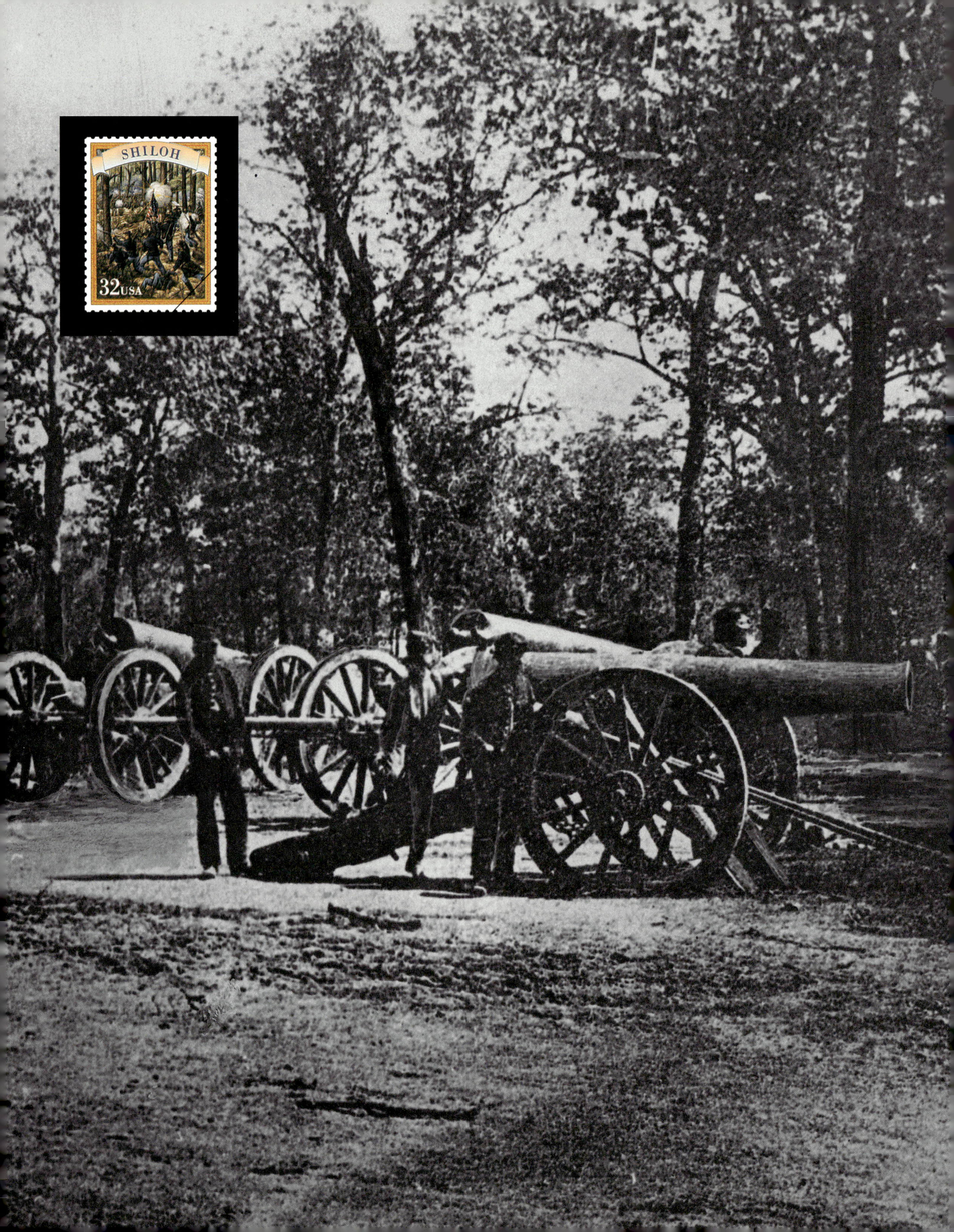
SHILOH
32USA

SHILOH
April 6-7, 1862

At dawn on April 6, 1862, Union army troops encamped around little Shiloh Church on a bluff of the Tennessee River at Pittsburg Landing were sleepily cooking their breakfast when they received the shock of a lifetime. Announcing themselves with fusillades of musket fire, hundreds of Rebel soldiers were spilling from the thickets and surging toward the Union tents. Screaming the fearsome Rebel yell, the Confederates overran the Yankee camps and sent the disorganized blue-clad troops in full flight toward the river.

The bold Rebel stroke was conceived by General Albert Sidney Johnston, who sought to retrieve Confederate fortunes in the West. In the first months of 1862, the loss of Forts Henry and Donelson to Northern troops led by a previously little-known general named U.S. Grant gave control of the Tennessee and Cumberland rivers to the Union. Johnston's army retreated to Corinth, Mississippi, abandoning Kentucky and Tennessee to the Yankees. Grant pursued, intending to attack the strategic rail hub of Corinth. Instead, it was Johnston who struck first, and his gambit came close to succeeding.

Watching his troops marching toward the enemy through a heavy white mist that dawn, Johnston predicted victory. "Tonight we will water our horses in the Tennessee River," he said. But the Federals recovered from their initial shock at Shiloh and managed to patch together a defensive position in a sunken road, a clump of forest and a peach orchard—a bloody perimeter known ever after as "the Hornet's Nest." The Rebels attacked again and again, only to be repulsed. Eventually the Hornet's Nest was captured, but the fighting proved costly. Leading an assault, General Johnston was nicked by a musket ball that severed an artery in his leg; he bled to death on the field. General P.G.T. Beauregard took command of the Confederate forces, but was unable to break the new Yankee line.

Grant, who was absent when the battle began, hastened back to Pittsburg Landing and took charge of his battered army. Massed Federal siege guns blunted a Rebel charge that evening, and Union reinforcements began to arrive. That night hundreds of wounded men lay moaning in a no man's land while lightning flashed and a cold rain fell. On April 7 Grant took the initiative away from Beauregard. Yankee troops pushed the Southern troops back to Shiloh Church, recaptured the camps, and won the most terrible battle yet fought in the war. More than 23,000 men had been killed, wounded or reported missing on those two bloody days. ♣

This bugle was shot from the hands of Frederick Barnhart, an Indiana private, as he was sounding the call to battle at Shiloh. He retrieved the instrument as a memento. Opposite, on a bluff near Pittsburg Landing, Illinois artillerymen stand at their guns a few days after the battle.

Brigadier General William T. Sherman *(left)* was praised as a "gallant and able officer" in the official report of the battle written by the Union commander, Ulysses S. Grant *(right)*. In the painting below, General Benjamin Prentiss, on horseback at right, directs Union troops defending the Hornet's Nest against one of the Confederate attacks on the afternoon of April 6, 1862.

Shortly before the battle, Confederate troops received a major shipment of British Enfield rifle muskets *(above)* that had been smuggled past the Union coastal blockade.

"The scenes on this field would have cured anyone of war."

Brigadier General William Tecumseh Sherman

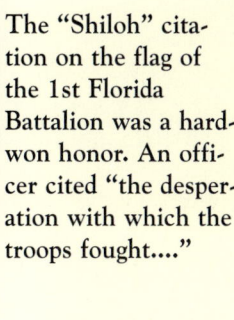

The "Shiloh" citation on the flag of the 1st Florida Battalion was a hard-won honor. An officer cited "the desperation with which the troops fought...."

This sketch shows Rebels streaming into the Union camp near Shiloh Church at dawn on April 6, 1862. Initially routed, the Federal troops regrouped.

The death of Albert Sidney Johnston *(left)* at Shiloh was considered a catastrophe in the South. General P.G.T. Beauregard *(right)* replaced the fallen Johnston as Confederate commander on the field.

★★★★★★★★★★★★ 1862 ★★★★★★★★★★★★

April 24 - Federal fleet under Farragut passes the forts below New Orleans, Louisiana.

April 25 - Surrender of New Orleans, Louisiana. Surrender of Fort Macon near Beaufort, North Carolina.

May 3 - Evacuation of Yorktown, Virginia, by Confederates.

May 5 - Battle of Williamsburg, Virginia.

May 8 - Battle of McDowell, Virginia.

May 9 - Evacuation of Norfolk by Confederates.

May 11 - C.S.S. *Virginia* burned to prevent capture.

May 15 - Battle of Drewry's Bluff, Virginia.

May 20 - Federal Homestead Law signed.

May 23 - Engagement at Front Royal, Virginia.

May 25 - Battle of Winchester, Virginia.

May 30 - Corinth, Mississippi, evacuated by Confederates.

May 31 - Battle of Fair Oaks (Seven Pines), Virginia. General Joseph E. Johnston wounded. General Robert E. Lee assumes command.

June 1 - Conclusion of the Battle of Fair Oaks (Seven Pines), Virginia.

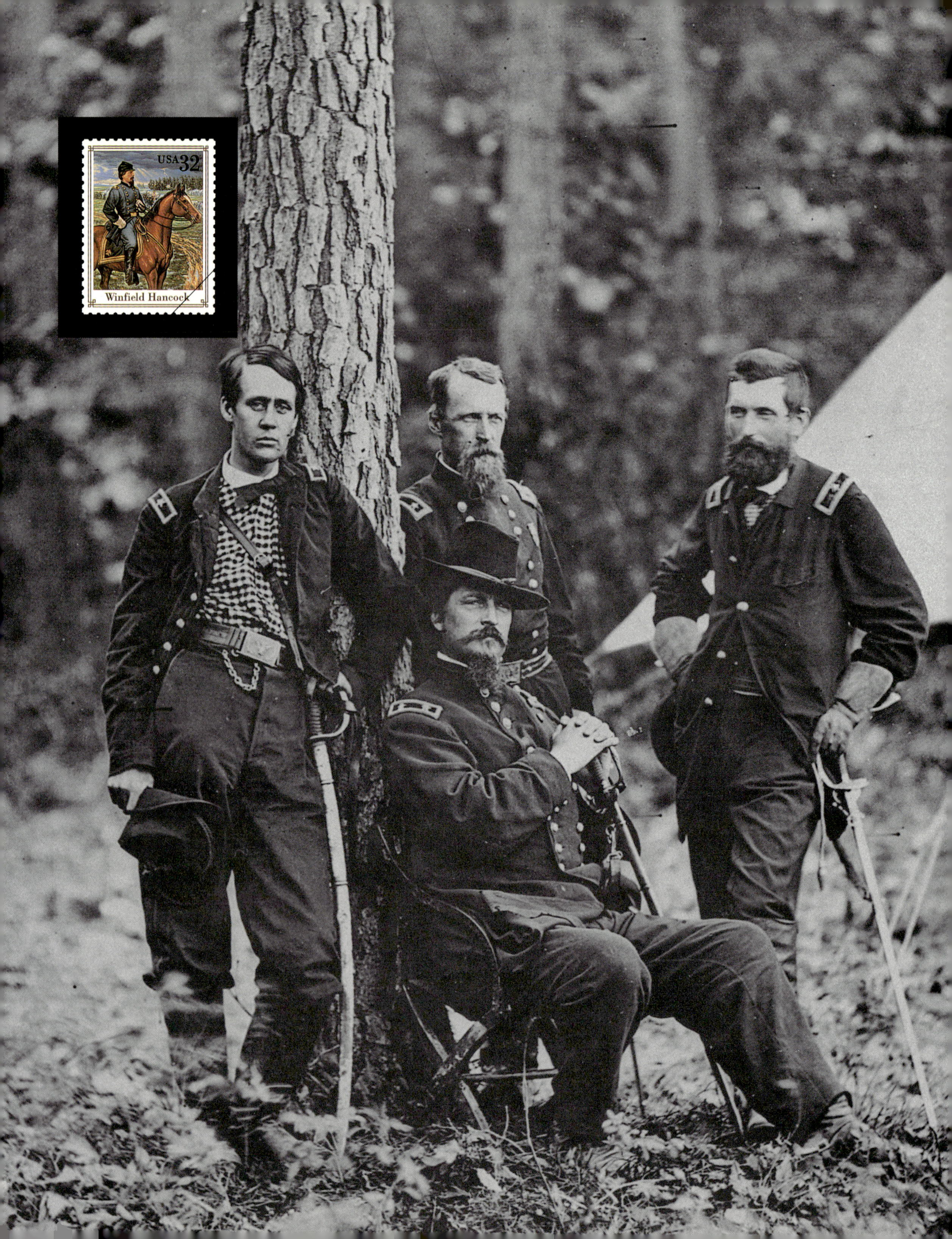
USA 32
Winfield Hancock

Winfield Scott Hancock
1824-1886

On the afternoon of May 5, 1862, five Federal regiments waited anxiously for their baptism of fire near the old colonial town of Williamsburg, Virginia. The bluecoats hunkered down amidst a drenching downpour, listening to the unmistakable roar of battle drawing closer until it drowned out the thunder of the storm.

A battle line of Southern troops appeared, the Rebels taunting their foes with shouts of "Bull Run!" The order came to open fire, and as the Union soldiers blazed away at the men in gray, their commander, Brigadier General Winfield Scott Hancock, shouted, "Gentlemen, charge with the bayonet!" The general spurred his horse alongside the cheering troops, and the Rebels gave way before the wall of bristling steel.

Army of the Potomac commander George McClellan credited his gallant subordinate with turning the tide of battle at Williamsburg, reporting that "Hancock was superb today." The praise seemed well suited to the tall, broad-shouldered Pennsylvanian, who would soon be known throughout the army as "Hancock the Superb."

Educated at West Point and a veteran of the Mexican War, Winfield Scott Hancock coupled organizational skills with an unparalleled ability to galvanize and inspire men in battle. His imposing physical presence, booming voice and spotless uniform made Hancock a model officer for young volunteer soldiers fighting in the Union's cause. "One felt safe when near him," a veteran remembered.

In December 1862, Hancock led a division in the doomed assault at Fredericksburg, and in May 1863 he covered the army's retreat at the Battle of Chancellorsville. His greatest service of the war came a month later at Gettysburg. As commander of the Second Corps Hancock staved off defeat on the first day of the battle, and for the next two days held the center of the Union line. On July 3 he was severely wounded during the repulse of the Confederate assault known as Pickett's Charge.

Hancock continued to serve in the U.S. Army in the decades following the war, and in 1880 narrowly lost a presidential campaign to James A. Garfield. At his death in 1886, "Hancock the Superb" was widely mourned as one of the Union's finest military commanders. ♣

This flag flew at the headquarters of Hancock's Second Corps. Among the division commanders supporting Hancock (*seated, opposite*) were the three men standing from left to right: Brigadier General Francis C. Barlow, Major General David D. Birney and Brigadier General John Gibbon.

Hancock's birthplace in Norristown, Pennsylvania

Hancock recuperating from Gettysburg wound

Above, Federals commanded by Gen
Winfield Scott Hancock *(on brown*
at left) repulse a Confederate attack
Williamsburg in May of 1862. The
ing year, Hancock fell gravely woun
Gettysburg *(left)*.

General Hancock after the war

An 1880 cartoon by Thomas Nast portrays Democratic presidential nominee Hancock *(right)* as an old soldier ignorant of the meaning of the word "tariff." Hancock's successful Republican opponent, James Garfield, was also a celebrated Union general.

★★★★★★★★★★★
1862
★★★★★★★★★★★

June 3-5 Evacuation of Fort Pillow, Tennessee, by Confederates.

June 6 - Battle of Memphis, Tennessee.

June 9 - Battle of Port Republic, Virginia.

June 16 - Engagement at Secessionville, South Carolina.

June 19 - Lincoln signs law prohibiting slavery in the territories.

June 25 - Beginning of the Seven Days' Battles before Richmond, Virginia.

June 26 - Battle of Mechanicsville (Beaver Dam Creek), Virginia.

June 27 - Battle of Gaines' Mill (First Cold Harbor), Virginia.

June 28 - Farragut's Federal fleet passes Vicksburg, Mississippi.

June 29 - Battle of Savage's Station, Virginia.

June 30 - Battle of Frayser's Farm (White Oak Swamp), Virginia.

July 1 - Battle of Malvern Hill, Virginia. Federal government passes Income Tax and Railroad acts.

July 2 - Land grant education system passed by U.S. government.

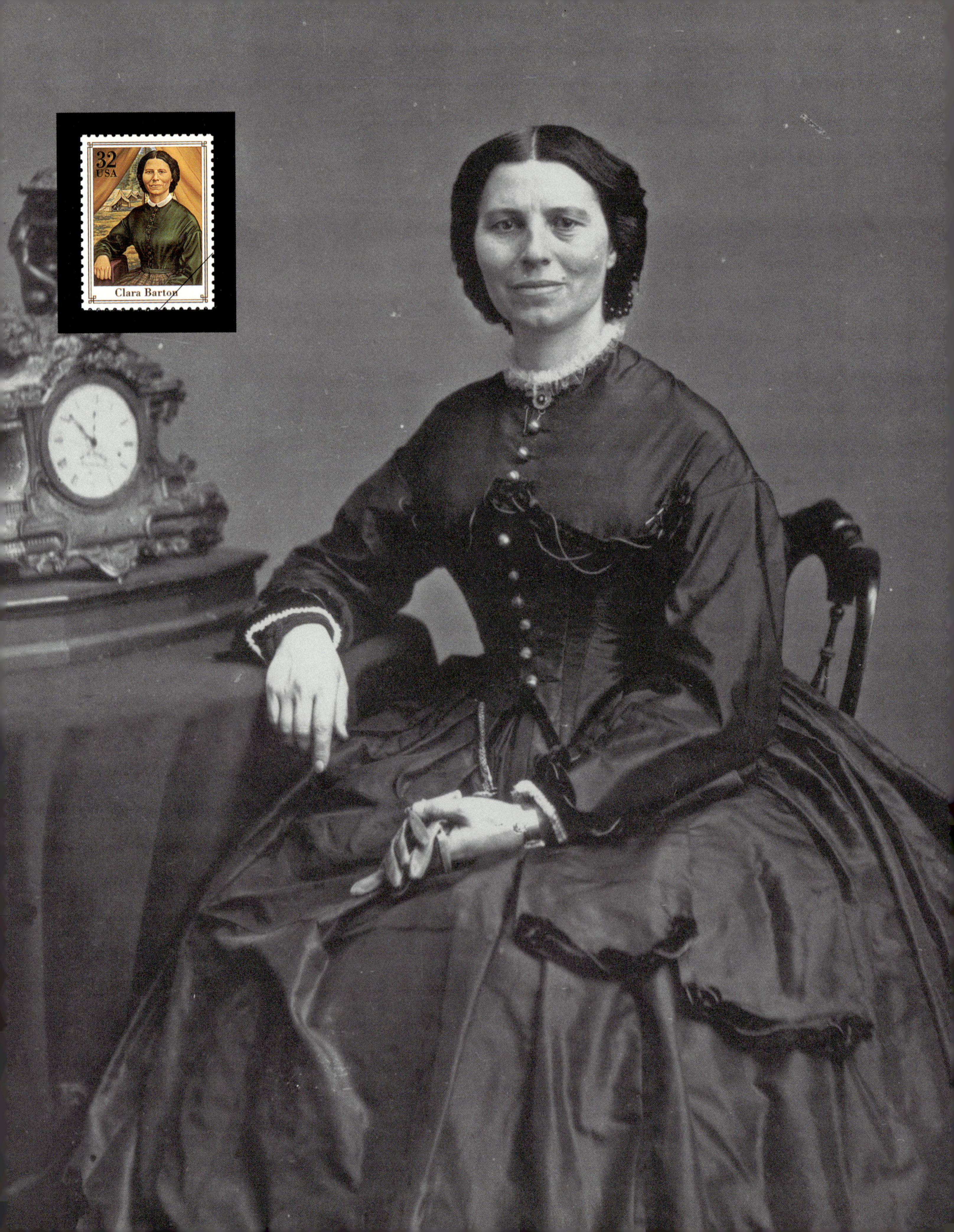
32
USA
Clara Barton

CLARA HARLOWE BARTON
1821-1912

The situation at the makeshift Union army field hospital in Culpeper, Virginia, following the August 1862 battle at Cedar Mountain was typical of the carnage left in the wake of every Civil War battle. Hundreds of shattered men wrapped in filthy bandages lay groaning in pools of their own blood. The air reeked of vomit and excrement, and the dead lay next to the dying amid piles of amputated limbs. Into this hellish scene, the small neat figure of Clara Barton appeared like an apparition. She had come from Washington, bringing fresh dressings, blankets, food and medicines, and as one exhausted surgeon later wrote to his wife, "if heaven ever sent out a homely angel, she must be one, her assistance was so timely."

This was the first time that 40-year old Clarissa Harlowe Barton had seen the horrors of war firsthand. The youngest daughter of a large Massachusetts family, she was a strong-minded, opinionated loner who was supporting herself as a copyist for the U.S. Patent Office in Washington, D.C., when the war broke out. Intensely patriotic, yet too independent to submit to the discipline of any sanctioned nursing organization, she threw herself into the war effort as a resourceful freelance. She tirelessly distributed provisions donated by New England women's groups to combat casualties flooding the capital's poorly equipped infirmaries. But she longed to serve closer to the action, and galvanized by the chaos she witnessed in Culpepper, set out to take an active role at the front. Obtaining battlefield passes from prominent political friends, Barton appeared in the thick of the fighting at some of the bloodiest confrontations of the war—ferrying a steady stream of desperately needed supplies to Antietam, Fredericksburg, the Wilderness, Spotsylvania and Petersburg. To beleaguered doctors, her fresh provisions were a godsend; to the wounded and dying men she cleaned, bandaged and comforted, she became a surrogate mother, sister and sweetheart. They called her the "Angel of the Battlefield." In 1865, drawing on the many letters she received and the battlefield connections she had made, she began to compile lists of dead and missing soldiers, eventually piecing together information about the fates of more than 13,000 Union prisoners who disappeared in the notorious Confederate prison at Andersonville, Georgia.

After the war, Clara Barton traveled in Europe, where she learned of a new relief organization, the International Red Cross. In 1881, she organized its American counterpart, serving as president until 1906. At her death in 1912 at the age of 91, Clara Barton was the most widely known and honored American woman of her generation. ☘

In 1882, the International Committee of the Red Cross awarded Clara Barton this medal for her efforts in shaping the American wing of the organization. Opposite, Barton poses for photographer Mathew Brady in 1865.

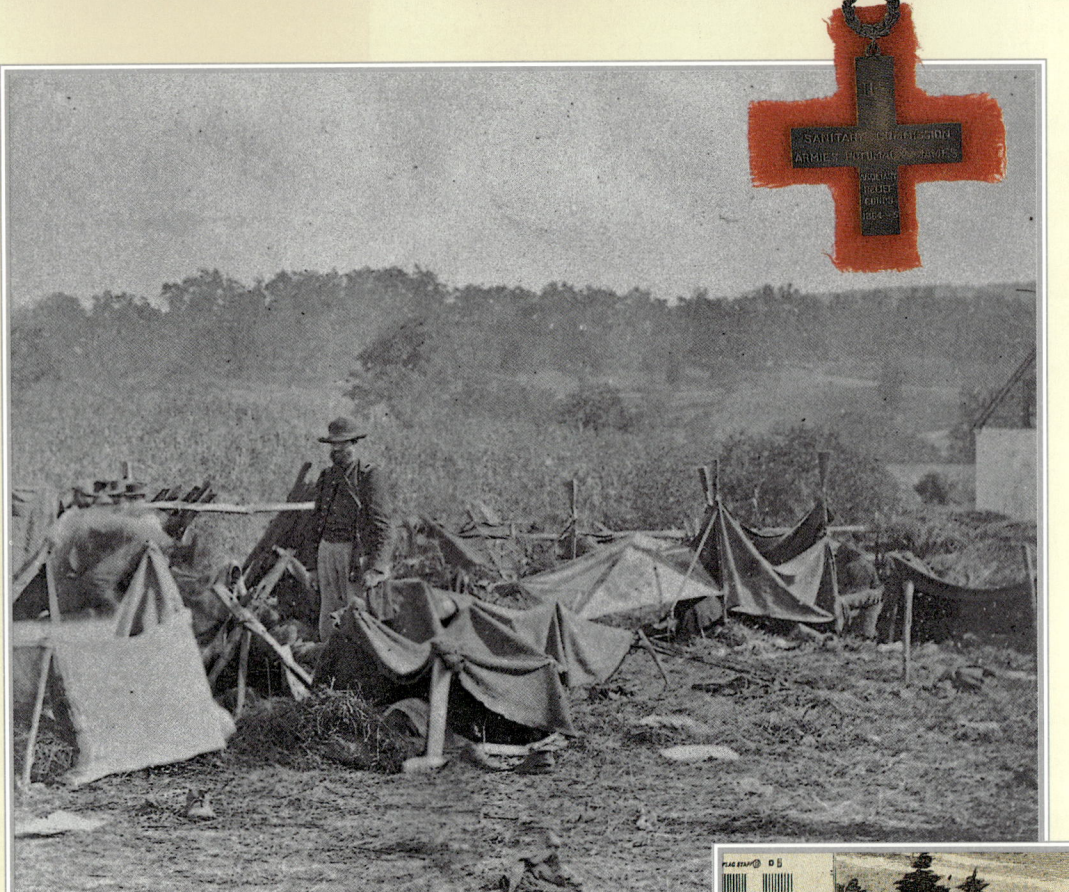

Confederate wounded are tended at a Federal field hospital at Antietam, where Clara Barton served close to the front lines. On one occasion a stray bullet passed through her sleeve, killing a soldier she held in her arms. For her service during the war, she was awarded the medal of the Sanitary Commission Armies of the Potomac and James Auxilliary Relief Corps *(inset)*.

In the *Harpers Weekly* engraving below, Clara Barton raises the flag at the dedication of Andersonville national cemetery on August 17, 1865. There she helped identify thousands of graves.

LECTURE!

MISS CLARA BARTON,
OF WASHINGTON,

THE HEROINE OF ANDERSONVILLE,

The Soldier's Friend, who gave her time and fortune during the war to the Union cause, and who is now engaged in searching for the missing soldiers of the Union army, will address the people of

LAMBERTVILLE, in

HOLCOMBE HALL,

THIS EVENING,
APRIL 7TH, AT 7½ O'CLOCK.
SUBJECT:

SCENES ON THE BATTLE-FIELD.
ADMISSION,   25 CENTS.

Clara Barton lectured on women's rights as well as her Civil War experiences. Plagued by bouts of nervousness and ill health, she nevertheless enjoyed her popularity as a public speaker.

Families wrote to Barton during the Civil War seeking her help in locating their loved ones.

Clara Barton carried this portable sewing kit called a "housewife" on the battlefield.

Built in 1891 from lumber salvaged from a Red Cross warehouse, Barton's house in Glen Echo, Maryland, was also the national headquarters of the American Red Cross. The double doors to her office *(right)* bear the emblem of the organization.

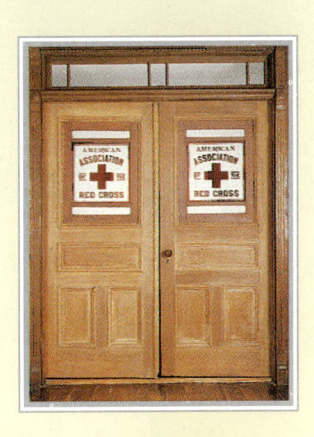

One of the most decorated women in United States history, Clara Barton wore her medals often, sometimes while gardening or milking her cows. Pictured are decorations from the following foreign states: Germany *(top and bottom left)*, Russia *(top center)*, Turkey *(bottom center)* and Armenia *(above)*.

In her eighth decade, Clara Barton wrote, "You have never known me without work, and you never will." She was 83 in this photograph.

1862

July 11 - Major General Henry W. Halleck appointed general-in-chief of U.S. armies.

July 15 - C.S.S. *Arkansas* attacks Federal fleet north of Vicksburg, Mississippi.

July 17 - Confiscation Act signed by Lincoln.

July 22 - Lincoln presents Emancipation Proclamation to cabinet.

August 2 - Engagement at Malvern Hill, Virginia.

August 5 - Engagement at Baton Rouge, Louisiana.

August 6 - C.S.S. *Arkansas* lost in action.

August 9 - Battle of Cedar Mountain, Virginia.

August 17 - Sioux uprising begins in Minnesota.

August 24 - C.S.S. *Alabama* commissioned off the Azores. Commander Raphael Semmes.

August 26 - Battle of Second Bull Run (Second Manassas), Virginia, begins.

August 28 - Battle of Groveton (Brawner's Farm), Virginia. Confederate army under Braxton Bragg enters Tennessee.

August 29-30 Battle of Second Bull Run (Second Manassas), Virginia.

September 1 - Battle of Chantilly (Ox Hill), Virginia.

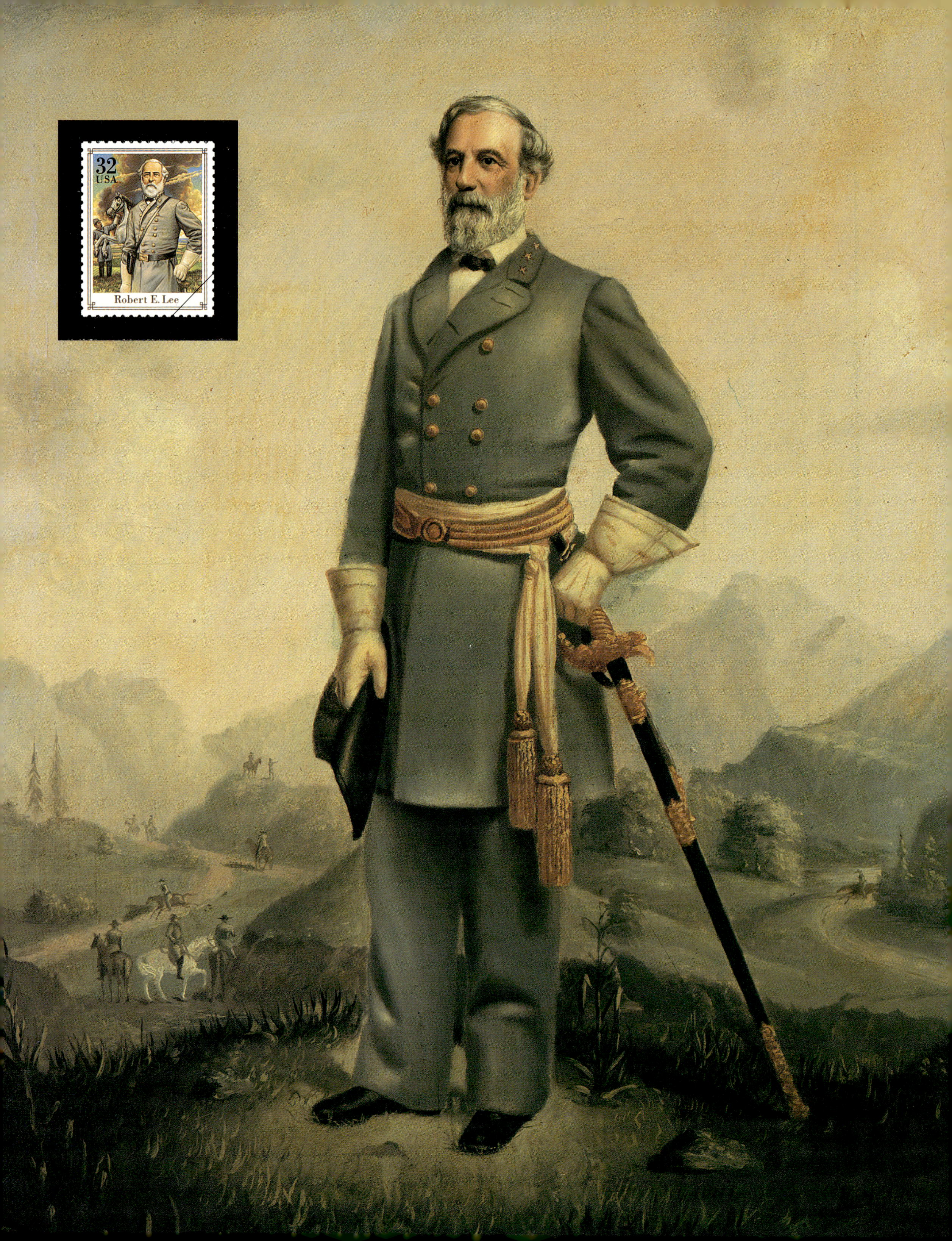
32
USA
Robert E. Lee

ROBERT EDWARD LEE
1807-1870

No veteran of the Army of Northern Virginia would ever forget his first sight of General Robert E. Lee. For Major Robert Stiles the encounter came in the early summer of 1862, not long after Lee had assumed command of the army he would lead to immortality. "A magnificent staff approached from the direction of Richmond, and riding at its head, superbly mounted, a born king among men," Stiles recalled. Virginia Military Institute cadet John S. Wise echoed Stiles' assessment. "It is impossible to speak of General Lee without seeming to deal in hyperbole," Wise wrote. "Robert E. Lee was incomparably the greatest-looking man I ever saw...the impression which that man made by his presence, and by his leadership, upon all who came in contact with him, can be described by no other term than that of grandeur."

Robert E. Lee was a man of aristocratic lineage. His father had been one of George Washington's favorite generals in the Revolution, and his wife, Mary Custis Lee, was Martha Washington's great-granddaughter. Lee performed so brilliantly in the Mexican War that the U.S. commander, Winfield Scott, called him "the very best soldier that I ever saw in the field." He later served as superintendent of West Point. Lee's distinguished record in the U.S. Army made him a logical choice for command of the forces being raised to suppress the Southern rebellion. But when that position was offered to him early in 1861, the 54-year-old colonel turned it down after much painful soul-searching. His strongest loyalty lay with his native state, Virginia, and Virginia had seceded from the Union and joined the Confederacy.

Lee took charge of the Army of Northern Virginia at the beginning of June 1862, and by the end of the month he had driven the Union forces from the outskirts of Richmond in the bloody Seven Days' Battles. Knowing the odds the Confederacy faced, Lee was ever willing to risk defeat to attain victory, and the Southern triumphs at Second Manassas and Chancellorsville testified to his tactical skill and daring strategy. Even after the repulse of the Confederates at Gettysburg, Lee's audacity, determination and ability to inspire his troops enabled the Army of Northern Virginia to fight on for nearly two more years.

Following the surrender at Appomattox, Lee served as president of Washington College—now known as Washington and Lee University. At his death in 1870 he was mourned by Northerners and Southerners alike as one of the greatest military commanders in the annals of American history. ♣

This cotton and wool bunting banner was used by Robert E. Lee as a headquarters flag during the early part of the War. It is possible that the flag, or at least its odd star arrangement, was sewn by the general's wife, Mary. The painting (*opposite*) portrays Lee at age 54.

Lee and his wife, Mary (*above*), made their home in her parents' estate in Arlington, Virginia (*below*), until war broke out. "Her thoughts were ever in the past at Arlington," said their youngest child, Mildred.

Eight-year-old Rooney leans on his father's shoulder in a daguerreotype made around 1845.

While stationed at Cockspur Island, Georgia, with the Corps of Engineers in 1830, Lee spent his off-duty hours writing letters, playing cards or chess, and sketching. He presented his drawings of an alligator and a diamondback terrapin to a young woman in nearby Savannah.

In one of the first war photographs, General John Wool (*left of center*) leads officers through Saltillo, Mexico, during the Mexican War in 1847. Lee, the engineer in charge of building roads and bridges for Wool, is thought to be among the group.

The 1862 photograph at right was the first picture of Lee taken after the Civil War broke out.

"If there is one man in either army, Confederate or Federal, head and shoulders above every other in audacity, it is General Lee. His name might be Audacity."

Colonel Joseph Ives, C.S.A.

Astride his gray mount Traveller, General Robert E. Lee pauses beneath an oak tree with his senior officers to reconnoiter an enemy position. The aggressive strategy Lee embraced after taking command of the Army of Northern Virginia in the spring of 1862 reversed for a time the tide of the Civil War in the eastern theater.

Photographed by Mathew Brady a week after the surrender at Appomattox, Robert E. Lee still wears his uniform. Standing beside him are his eldest son, Major General George Washington Custis Lee *(far left)*, and Lieutenant Colonel Walter H. Taylor, a longtime aide. Lee's wartime gear *(right)* is displayed on his camp table.

Lee in January 1870, the last year of his life. The four-cent stamp with Lee and Stonewall Jackson was issued in 1937.

Mourners crowd around the Washington College chapel for Lee's funeral.

1862

September 14 - Battles of South Mountain and Crampton's Gap, Maryland.

September 15 - Confederates under General Thomas J. Jackson capture Harpers Ferry, Virginia.

September 17 - Battle of Antietam (Sharpsburg), Maryland. Capture of Munfordsville, Kentucky, by Confederates.

September 19 - Battle of Iuka, Mississippi.

September 22 - Emancipation Proclamation announced.

October 3-4 Battle of Corinth, Mississippi.

October 8 - Battle of Perryville, Kentucky.

December 7 - Battle of Prairie Grove, Arkansas.

December 13 - Battle of Fredericksburg, Virginia.

December 20 - Confederate raid against Holly Springs, Mississippi.

December 29 - Battle of Chickasaw Bayou, Mississippi.

December 31 - Battle of Stones River (Murfreesboro), Tennessee. State of West Virginia admitted to the Union.

1863

January 1 - Emancipation Proclamation issued.

January 2 - Second day, Battle of Stones River (Murfreesboro), Tennessee.

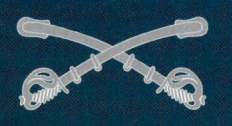

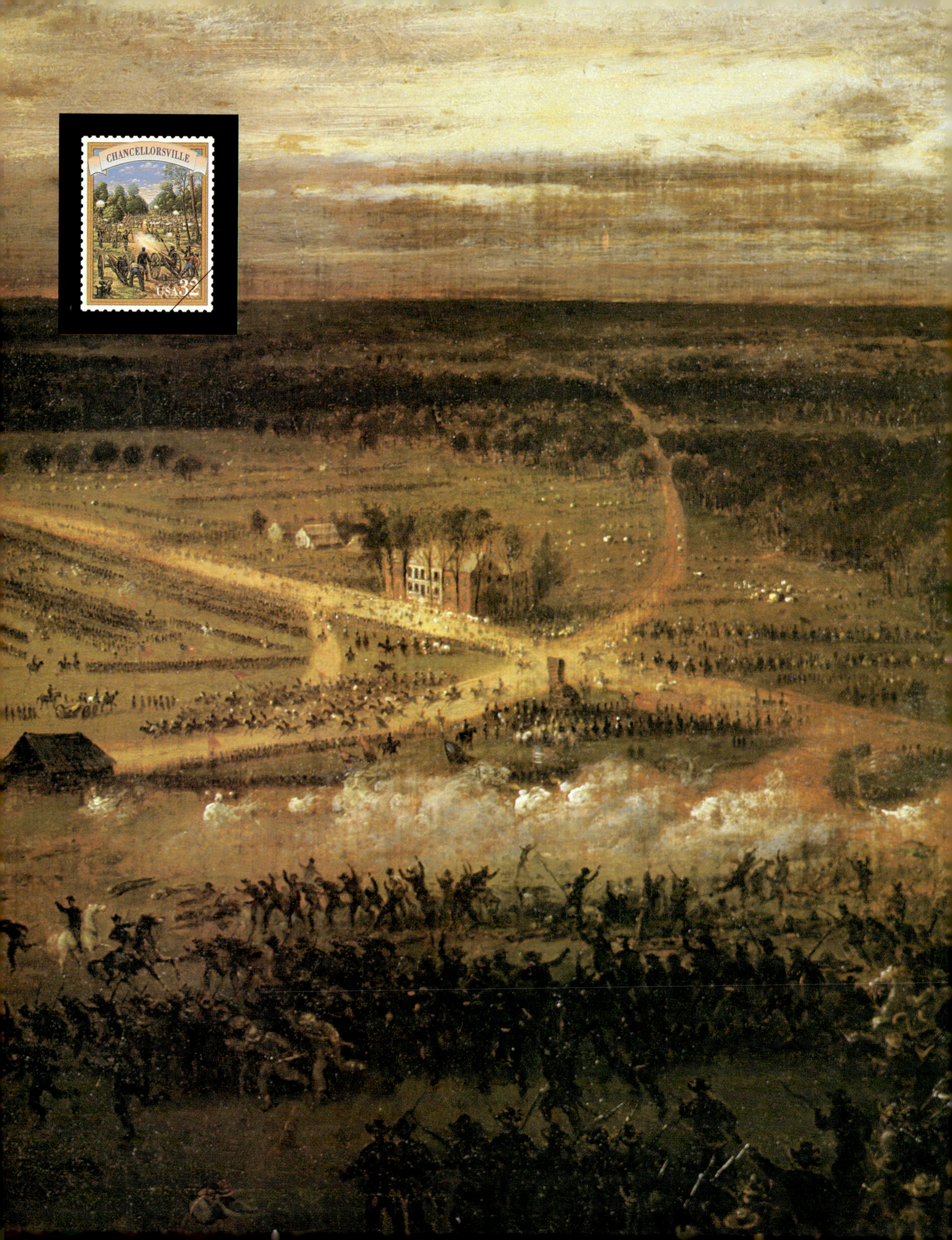
CHANCELLORSVILLE
USA 32

CHANCELLORSVILLE
May 1-4, 1863

On the evening of May 1, 1863, the Confederacy's two greatest commanders, Robert E. Lee and Thomas J. "Stonewall" Jackson, conferred beside a campfire in the tangled Virginia forest known as the Wilderness. After months of inactivity both Lee's Army of Northern Virginia and Major General Joseph Hooker's Army of the Potomac were on the move, jockeying for position before inevitably locking in battle. Though foiled in the past, the Yankee army and its self-confident commander seemed to have the upper hand this time. "Fighting Joe" Hooker had managed to march approximately 70,000 troops around the Confederate left flank to the Wilderness crossroads of Chancellorsville, where he was in a position to strike at the rear of Lee's army, which was encamped at nearby Fredericksburg.

But after some inconclusive skirmishing, Hooker had inexplicably failed to strike. He remained at Chancellorsville, digging in and waiting for Lee's next move. Though the Yankees had 30,000 more men than Lee did, the Southern leader and his top lieutenant decided on a risky and bold course of action—to strike first and count on surprise and maneuver to carry the day. Shortly after dawn of May 2, Jackson led 26,000 troops on a circuitous, 10-mile march along narrow woodland paths to a position opposite the Federal right flank.

Just before sunset, Jackson's battle lines surged down upon the unsuspecting Yankees, smashed through their defenses, and drove them eastward in demoralized retreat. Nightfall, the wooded terrain, and stiffening Union resistance eventually slowed the Southern onslaught, but the attack had been wildly successful. The Confederates' elation was tempered, however, by the tragic wounding of Stonewall himself—mistakenly fired upon by his own men as he rode through their ranks in the gloom.

Despite the loss of his most trusted subordinate, Robert E. Lee continued his offensive on May 3, forcing the Federals into an ever-shrinking perimeter at Chancellorsville. In the course of the fighting Hooker was stunned by an exploding artillery shell, and temporarily disabled. Facing disaster, the Union troops ultimately evacuated their position and retreated across the Rappahannock River.

At a cost of more than 17,000 men killed, wounded or captured, the Union had suffered yet another defeat at the hands of Robert E. Lee. But the nearly 13,000 Confederates lost at Chancellorsville included Stonewall Jackson, who died of his wounds eight days after his daring march had put the Federals to flight. ♣

This Confederate battle flag was captured at Chancellorsville on May 3 by the 7th New York Volunteers. Opposite: A fanciful painting of the battle at sunset on May 2 shows the red brick Chancellor House as the nucleus of swirling thrust and counter-thrust.

45

A Rebel brigade storms a Federal breastwork on the turnpike west of Chancellorsville, taking Union defenders by surprise.

Union infantry and reserve artillery man breastwork north of Chancellorsville on May 2, 1863, in this sketch by Edwin Forbes. The smoke of battle can be seen rising above the tree line.

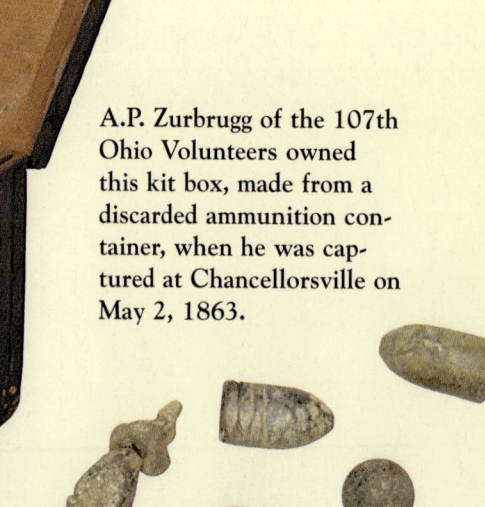

A.P. Zurbrugg of the 107th Ohio Volunteers owned this kit box, made from a discarded ammunition container, when he was captured at Chancellorsville on May 2, 1863.

Rifle and musket projectiles found at Chancellorsville

Major General Joseph Hooker

"Turn right or left, grim death stared at us. The heavens seemed filled with hot-breathed, shrieking demons."

Captain Charles H. Weygant, 124th New York Infantry, U.S.A.

Stonewall Jackson and his staff

This torn notebook, open to a sketch of Banks' Ford on the Rappahannock River, was carried by Captain James Boswell, Jackson's trusted 24-year-old chief engineer. The slender book failed to stop the bullet that killed Boswell; in the same volley, Jackson was mortally wounded.

The ruins of the once-imposing Chancellor House testify to the fury of the fighting.

★★★★★★★★★★★★
1 8 6 3
★★★★★★★★★★★★

January 11 - Arkansas post (Fort Hindman) captured by Federals.

January 22 - Burnside's "Mud March" fails.

January 31 - Confederate ironclads *Chicora* and *Palmetto State* interrupt the Federal blockade of Charleston Harbor, South Carolina.

February 25 - Federal Congress sets up national bank system and passes an act to establish a national currency. Conscription act passed.

March 14 - Federal gunboats pass Port Hudson, Louisiana.

March 17 - Battle of Kelly's Ford, Virginia.

April 3 - Bread riots in Richmond.

April 7 - Unsuccessful Federal naval attack on Charleston, South Carolina.

April 11 - Confederates under General James Longstreet besiege Suffolk, Virginia.

April 16 - Admiral David D. Porter's Federal fleet passes Vicksburg.

April 17 - Grierson's raid into Mississippi begins.

May 1-4 Battle of Chancellorsville, Virginia. "Stonewall" Jackson wounded on May 1.

May 3 - Second Battle of Fredericksburg and Battle of Salem Church, Virginia. Longstreet abandons the siege of Suffolk, Virginia.

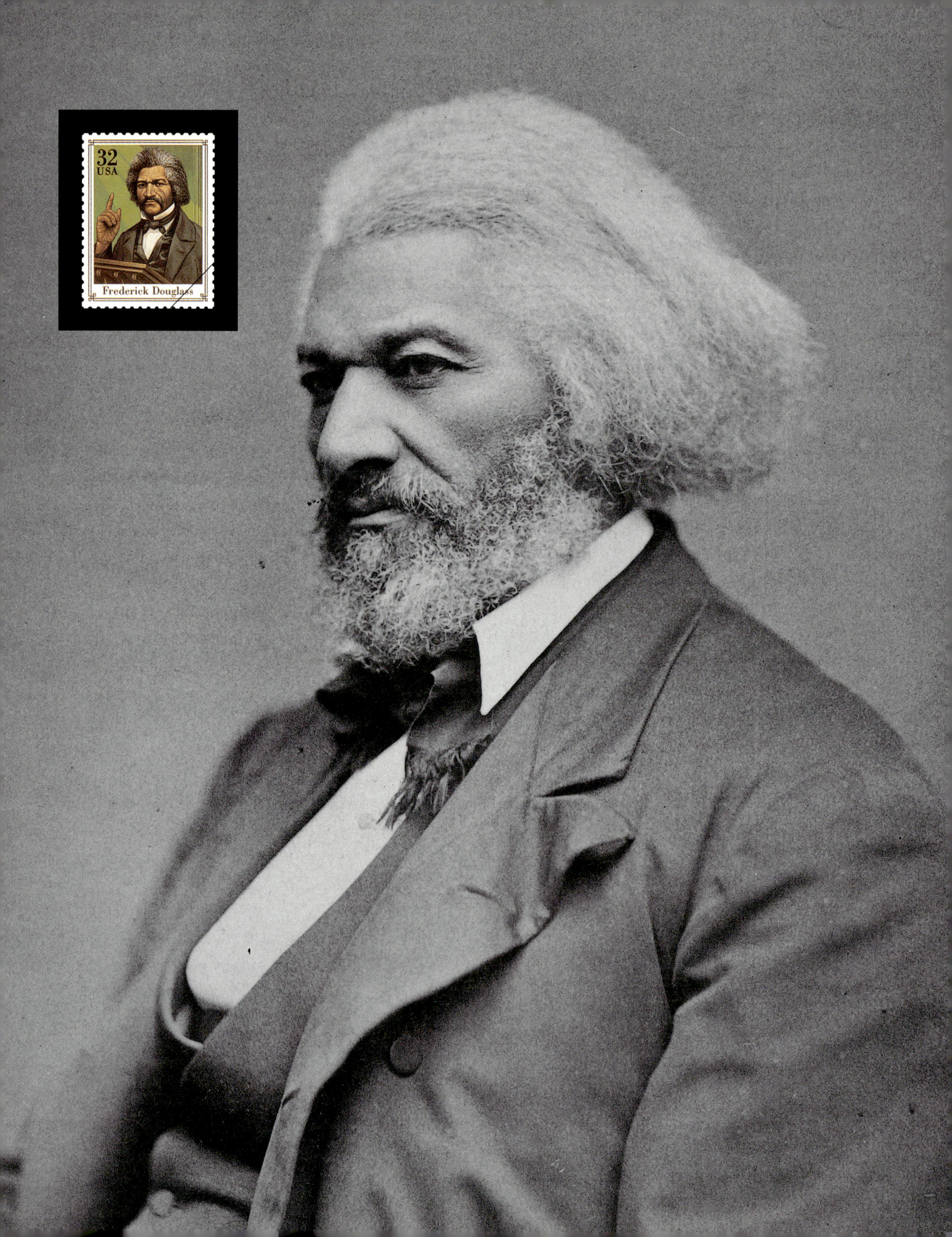
32
USA
Frederick Douglass

FREDERICK DOUGLASS
c.1817-1895

He was "majestic in his wrath," wrote feminist Elizabeth Cady Stanton of Frederick Douglass, the abolitionist whose impassioned oratory and forceful writing on human injustice made him the most famous African American of the 19th century. Douglass was born a slave, named Frederick Bailey, on a plantation in Tuckahoe, Maryland. In 1825, when he was about seven years old, he was sent to work as a houseboy in Baltimore. Defying the law, his mistress there taught him to read and write until her husband put a stop to the lessons, declaring they would make the boy unfit "to be a slave." But the precocious youngster had already concluded that in literacy lay "the pathway from slavery to freedom." He continued to teach himself secretly, bribing Baltimore street urchins for help by giving them scraps from his own meager meals.

At 21, posing as a sailor, he escaped north, where he took the name Douglass to conceal his origins. In 1841, speaking extemporaneously before abolitionists in a Nantucket hall, Douglass so electrified the crowd that he was hired on the spot as a full-time speaker for the Massachusetts Anti-Slavery Society. Relating his own experiences in a deep melodious voice, the tall, strikingly handsome figure was an immediate sensation on the lecture circuit, a speaker whose eloquence and moral authority would bring him international fame as one of the greatest orators in a golden age of oratory.

Douglass was forced to flee the United States in 1845, when the publication of his best-selling autobiography exposed his identity as the fugitive Frederick Bailey. When he returned two years later, his freedom having been purchased by British reformers, he founded the abolitionist newspaper, the *North Star*. Douglass was widely recognized as the nation's preeminent black spokesman. When the Civil War broke out, he lobbied Lincoln to make emancipation a primary goal of the conflict. After the Emancipation Proclamation was signed in 1863, Douglass served as a recruiting agent, enlisting scores of black soldiers into the Union army.

After the war, Douglass received presidential appointments to several high civil service posts and served as minister and consul general to Haiti. A humanist who believed that "all great reforms go together," Douglass in later years lent his prestige to a host of social causes from female suffrage to prison reform. He died of a heart attack on February 20, 1895, only hours after returning to his Washington, D.C., home from speaking at a women's rights convention. ♣

According to the inscription on its gold head, this ebony walking stick was given to Frederick Douglass in 1890 by the Wayman Grove Camp Meeting Association. Opposite: Douglass, an ex-slave turned ship caulker, orator, public servant, statesman, and later called the "father of the civil rights movement," was showered with such honors and memorabilia in his later years.

Anna Murray, the free woman who funded Douglass' escape, became his wife and bore him five children in 44 years of marriage.

Two years after he was widowed, Douglass sparked criticism by marrying Helen Pitts, a white woman who worked as his secretary. He defended the marriage by claiming it proved that whites and blacks could live in complete equality under one roof.

A somber Frederick Douglass after he won early fame as a passionate orator and an abolitionist writer.

Purchased in Ireland in 1846 during his first lecture tour abroad, this silver pocket watch was Douglass' first timepiece and one he carried with him all his life.

In this photograph *(right)* from the 1840s, philanthropist Gerrit Smith *(at center)* speaks at an anti-slavery rally; seated before him is Douglass, the fugitive slave turned abolitionist orator. Some 50 years later, Douglass *(below)* works in his Washington, D.C., home.

On March 2, 1863, Douglass published his rousing, impassioned appeal *(left)* to blacks to take up arms for the Union. Spurred by their father's zeal, Douglass' sons Lewis Henry and Charles Redmond *(pictured right, in uniform)* joined the 54th Massachusetts Volunteers.

Frederick Douglass receives black well-wishers *(left)* as the new U.S. marshal of Washington, D.C., a post that enabled him to increase the number of black civil servants.

★★★★★★★★★★★★
1863
★★★★★★★★★★★★

May 10 - Death of General Thomas J. "Stonewall" Jackson.

May 12 - Engagement at Raymond, Mississippi.

May 14 - Engagement at Jackson, Mississippi.

May 16 - Battle of Champion's Hill, Mississippi.

May 17 - Engagement at Big Black River, Mississippi.

May 18 - Siege of Vicksburg, Mississippi, begins.

May 19 - First assault on Vicksburg.

May 21 - Siege of Port Hudson begins.

May 22 - Second assault on Vicksburg.

May 27 - First assault on Port Hudson, Louisiana.

June 9 - Battle of Brandy Station, Virginia.

June 14 - Battle of Second Winchester, Virginia. Second assault on Port Hudson, Louisiana.

June 15 - Battle of Winchester (Stephenson's Depot), Virginia.

June 23 - Tullahoma campaign begins in Tennessee.

July 1-3 Battle of Gettysburg, Pennsylvania.

July 4 - Surrender of Vicksburg, Mississippi.

July 8 - Surrender of Port Hudson, Louisiana.

Raphael Semmes

RAPHAEL SEMMES
1809-1877

As a Confederate raider on the high seas, Raphael Semmes fulfilled to the letter the mission assigned him in 1861: to inflict on the enemy's commerce "the greatest injury in the shortest time." For three years, he haunted shipping lanes from the North Atlantic to the South China Sea, capturing or destroying 82 U.S. merchant vessels with a combined value of more than $6 million. Frustrated Yankees branded him a pirate, but to Southerners he was an inspiration—a David stinging the Union Goliath.

Born in Maryland, Semmes joined the U.S. Navy as a midshipman at the age of 16 and later served as an officer in the Mexican War. A resident of Mobile, Alabama, when the state seceded, he was quick to cast his lot with the Confederacy. He began preying on Yankee merchantmen as skipper of the *Sumter*, a converted packet steamer with a pivoting cannon and four howitzers. In August 1862, he was promoted to captain and entrusted with a swift new vessel designed for commerce raiding: the steam-powered sloop *Alabama*, replete with eight guns and plenty of room to hold the captured cargo and crews Semmes took aboard before he burned or boarded their ships. He tried out the *Alabama* on the Yankee whaling fleet in the Azores that September and claimed 10 vessels in two weeks, enhancing his notoriety among Northerners.

Known as Old Beeswax for his shiny handlebar mustache, Semmes attracted able officers but had to put up with a motley crew, recruited from foreign ports or captured ships. "I have a precious set of rascals on board," he complained, "faithless in the matter of abiding by contracts, liars, thieves, and drunkards."

The *Alabama* at first faced little opposition from Union warships, which were preoccupied with blockading Southern ports. But Semmes goaded the Federals when he sank the gunboat *Hatteras* off Texas in January 1863. In June 1864, the U.S.S. *Kearsarge* cornered the *Alabama* while she was refitting at Cherbourg, France. Semmes gamely rode out under French escort into international waters to meet the better-armed and better-manned *Kearsarge*, which made quick work of the *Alabama*, sending the sloop and more than 20 of her crew to the bottom.

Semmes survived the sinking and was arrested by the Federals at war's end. He was eventually paroled by President Andrew Jackson, but only after spending four months in prison while a military commission sought grounds for trying him as a pirate. In truth, he was simply one of the most daring players in a contest that pitted Rebel and Yankee sailors on the world's high seas. ♣

Captain Raphael Semmes appears as a pirate, flaunting a cutlass and the Jolly Roger, in this caricature by Northern satirist Thomas Nast. The jaunty Semmes overtook scores of Union merchant ships aboard his fleet commerce raider, *Alabama* (*opposite*).

Semmes *(seated at center above)* appears with the officers of his first commerce raider, the converted merchant steamer *Sumter (left)*. "Her lines were easy and graceful," Semmes wrote fondly of the ship, "and she had a sort of saucy air about her."

Semmes' tattered navy cap *(right)* originally bore three stars above the anchor designating his captain's rank.

After being bested by the U.S.S. *Kearsarge* off Cherbourg, France, on June 19, 1864, the *Alabama* sinks stern first in a painting by French Impressionist Edouard Manet. Among the relics salvaged from the *Alabama* was the ship's wheel ring, engraved with a motto in French that summed up Semmes' wartime exploits: "God helps those who help themselves." Semmes *(above right)*, wearing the uniform of a captain, returned to Richmond and command of the James River Squadron in January 1865. He was made a rear admiral the following month.

> "Chasing a sail is very much like pursuing a coy maiden, the very coyness sharpening the pursuit."
>
> *Captain Raphael Semmes, C.S.N.*

✯✯✯✯✯✯✯✯✯✯
1863
✯✯✯✯✯✯✯✯✯✯

July 10 - Siege of Battery Wagner begins in Charleston Harbor, South Carolina.

July 11 - First assault on Battery Wagner, Charleston.

July 13 - Draft riots in New York City.

July 18 - Second assault on Battery Wagner, Charleston, South Carolina.

July 26 - Confederate general John H. Morgan and his raiders captured in Ohio.

August 17 - Federal fleet bombards Fort Sumter, Charleston Harbor, South Carolina.

August 21 - Confederate guerrillas sack Lawrence, Kansas.

September 6 - Confederates evacuate Battery Wagner and Morris Island, Charleston Harbor, South Carolina.

September 8 - Confederates turn back Federal gunboats at Sabine Pass, Texas.

September 10 - Federals capture Little Rock, Arkansas.

September 19-20 Battle of Chickamauga, Georgia.

October 5 - Confederate "David" torpedo boats attack Federal ships in Charleston Harbor, South Carolina.

October 9-22 Bristoe Station Campaign, Virginia.

October 13 - Grant appointed to command Military District of the Mississippi.

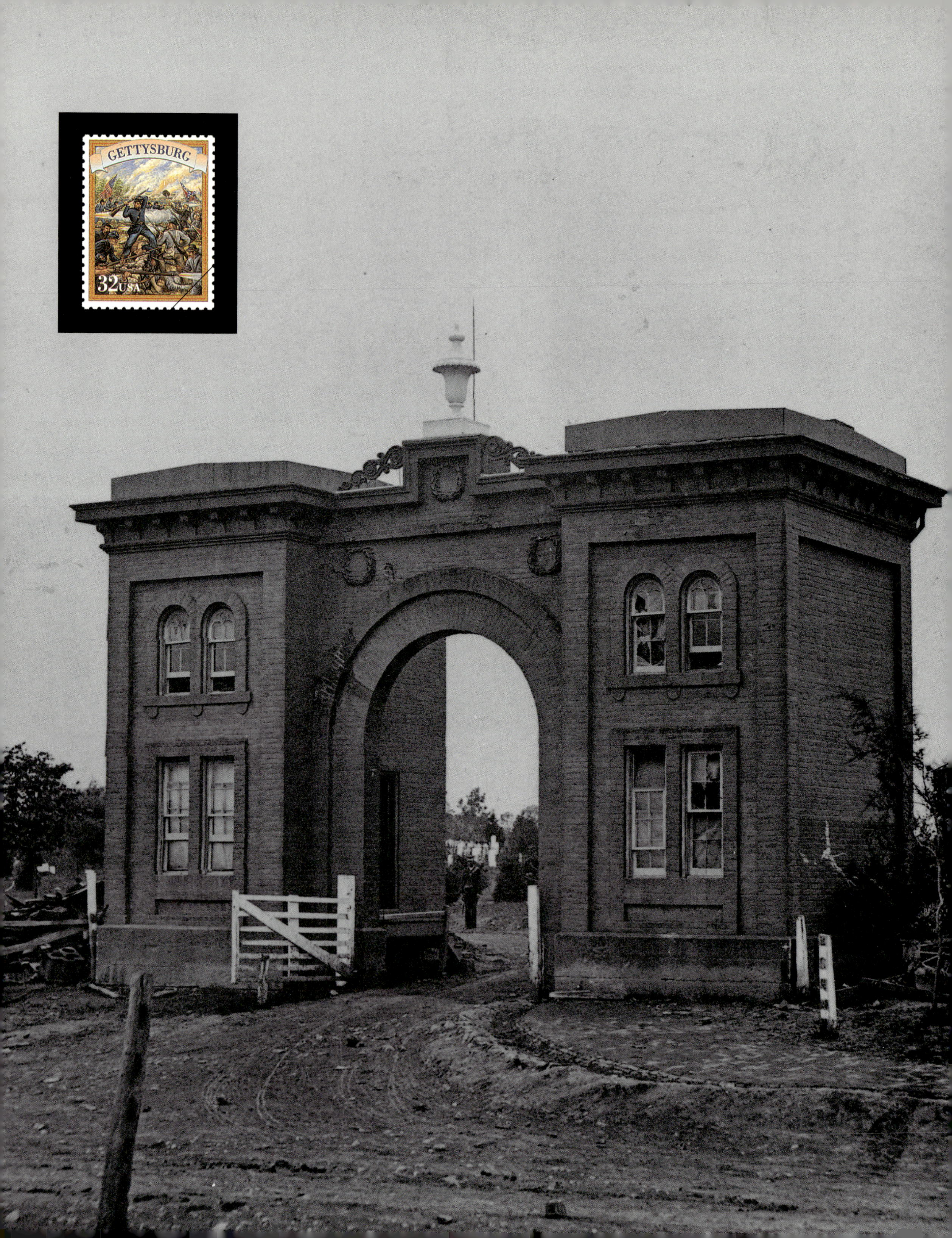
GETTYSBURG
32USA

GETTYSBURG
July 1-3, 1863

In the wake of the Confederate victory at Chancellorsville, General Robert E. Lee decided upon a daring gambit. For the second time in the span of less than a year, Lee's Army of Northern Virginia would launch an invasion of the North. If the Rebels could win a battle on soil occupied by the Northerners, perhaps the Federal government would sue for peace. On June 24, 1863, the Southern columns began crossing the Potomac River into Maryland, headed for Pennsylvania.

The Union Army of the Potomac had to march hard to catch up, but by the end of June the troops were closing in on Lee's forces. The inevitable confrontation came on July 1 at the little Pennsylvania town of Gettysburg. Twelve roads converged there, making it a logical point of concentration for both armies. When Rebel troops approached the town in search of badly needed shoes, they collided with members of the Union cavalry, and the greatest battle of the Civil War commenced.

Two corps of Yankee infantry arrived in time to slow the Confederate attack, but Lee brought more troops into action and by the end of July 1 succeeded in pushing the Federals back through Gettysburg to high ground south of the town. General George Meade, the Federal commander, arrived that night with most of his army, and occupied a strong defensive position shaped like a fishhook: from Culp's Hill to Cemetery Hill, and down the low spine of Cemetery Ridge to a rocky elevation called Little Round Top.

Lee maintained the initiative on the afternoon of July 2, launching General James Longstreet's corps in a series of sledgehammer blows that smashed a way through the Federal center. But Yankee counterattacks plugged up the gaps, and the Rebels failed to take the crucial height of Little Round Top. Unwilling to call off the attack, on July 3 Lee ordered Longstreet to attack Meade's center with the divisions of Generals Pickett, Pettigrew and Trimble. Following a massive artillery barrage, the Southern infantry charged toward Union troops defending a low stone wall along Cemetery Ridge. Only a handful of Rebels got there. With his hat on the tip of his sword, Brigadier General Lewis Armistead shouted, "Give them the cold steel!" and led 150 Virginians over the wall. The Yankees held, and with Armistead and most of his followers dead, dying or prisoners, the Southern effort to win the war at Gettysburg had failed. It was the high tide of Confederate hopes for independence, and with more than 50,000 casualties, the bloodiest battle in American history. ♣

Men of the 11th Mississippi Infantry Regiment charged with this flag to the stone wall that marked the Federal lines before being turned back on July 3, 1863, the last day of the battle. Opposite, the gatehouse of Gettysburg's Evergreen Cemetery, its windows smashed by bullets, stands on the crest of Cemetery Hill.

In the chaos on Cemetery Hill on the first day of battle, an exploding Rebel shell sends Union artillery horses crashing to the ground.

This sketch by Alfred Waud depicts the mortal wounding of General John Reynolds, an admired Union officer who was shot from the saddle during the initial action on July 1.

The 2d Massachusetts Volunteers carried this flag into battle at Gettysburg.

General James Longstreet, whom Robert E. Lee fondly called "my old warhorse," disagreed with his commander over tactics at Gettysburg but the two remained fast friends. Longstreet later wrote, "There was never a harsh word between us."

Colonel Joshua Chamberlain left a professorship at Maine's Bowdoin College to serve in the Union army, eventually taking command of the 20th Maine. His bold counterattack on Little Round Top won him the Medal of Honor.

This unfinished map of Gettysburg shows the town and the northern part of the battlefield.

Confederates *(background)* charge up Culp's Hill on the morning of July 3.

59

The flamboyant Major General George Pickett was one of three division commanders leading the Confederate attack on July 3. Nevertheless, the doomed offensive came to be known as "Pickett's Charge."

In this view of Pickett's Charge, embattled Federals strive to hold their ground while fresh troops charge to their relief at right.

The accurate Parrott rifle was used by both sides.

This painting depicts the Rebel charge at its height on July 3.

Three captive Confederates stand beside a breastwork atop Seminary Ridge, shortly before going off to a prison camp. They were among 5,425 unwounded soldiers captured by Meade's army; another 6,802 wounded fell into Federal hands. Below, Union dead litter a trampled field as a burial detail gathers in the distance.

"It is all over now. Many of us are prisoners, many are dead, many wounded, bleeding and dying. Your soldier lives and mourns and but for you, my darling, he would rather be back there with his dead, to sleep for all time in an unknown grave."

Major General George Pickett, C.S.A.

★★★★★★★★★★★
1 8 6 3
★★★★★★★★★★★

October 27 - Confederate siege of Chattanooga, Tennessee, broken.

November 19 - Lincoln's Gettysburg Address.

November 23-25 Battles for Chattanooga, Tennessee.

November 24 - Battle of Lookout Mountain, Chattanooga, Tennessee.

November 25 - Battle of Missionary Ridge, Chattanooga, Tennessee.

November 26 - Mine Run campaign begins in Virginia.

November 29 - Confederates attack Fort Sanders near Knoxville, Tennessee.

December 8 - Lincoln issues Proclamation of Amnesty and Reconstruction.

December 16 - General Joseph E. Johnston assumes command of Army of Tennessee.

1864

February 14 - Federals capture Meridian, Mississippi.

February 17 - Confederate submersible *Hunley* sinks U.S.S. *Housatanic* off Charleston Harbor, South Carolina.

February 20 - Battle of Olustee (Ocean Pond), Florida.

February 22 - Engagement at Okolona, Mississippi.

March 1 - Kilpatrick/Dahlgren raid on Richmond fails.

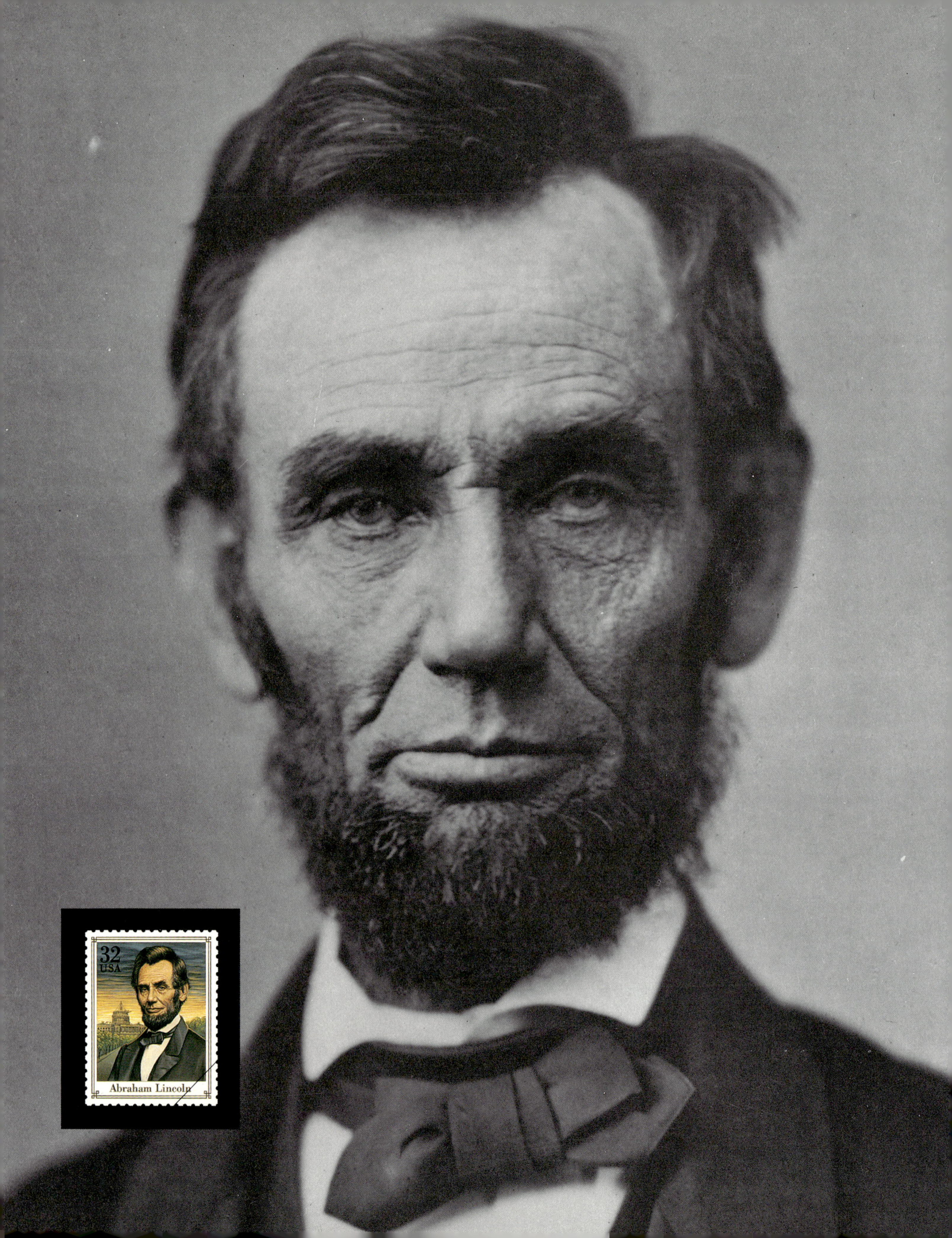
32
USA
Abraham Lincoln

ABRAHAM LINCOLN
1809-1865

"A house divided itself cannot stand," Abraham Lincoln declared in 1858. "I believe this government cannot endure permanently, half slave and half free. I do not expect the Union to be dissolved—I do not expect the house to fall—but I do expect it will cease to be divided." The 16th president's perception of such verities, and his eloquence in expressing them, were among the strengths that made Lincoln the nation's ideal leader in its time of severest test. Yet his formal schooling did not exceed a year; he was a self-taught man who had walked miles for books. He was not conventionally handsome, with his craggy head topping a six-foot-four frame, long gangly arms often encased in sleeves that seemed too short and legs in trousers with cuffs floating high above his scuffed boots. But when he arose to address America's hopes, fears or fundamental commitments, his was a figure of compelling gravity.

His presidency was trouble-plagued from the start. When he was elected in 1860, 10 Southern states gave him not a single popular vote. Before his inauguration in February 1861, secessionist states had organized the Confederacy, and a number of United States military commanders had defected, laying claim to their forts. Lincoln said he had no plans to interfere in the states, but had to preserve the union and would use his federal power to "hold, occupy, and possess" federal establishments. If something had to be done, he said, "I must do it."

Constantly searching for adequate commanders once the war began, he yearned for a "school of events" where men could try their hands before being tested by reality. His indulgent forebearance at times seemed more than his strutting generals deserved. After the arrogant George McClellan snubbed his commander in chief, Lincoln chose to overlook it, saying it was better "not to be making points of personal dignity." Only when McClellan ignored a chance to crush Lee's army after the Battle of Antietam did Lincoln replace him. And so it went, through general after general until he found men who could win. After they did win, the president pleaded that the victors forego vengeance. Likening a Southern state's new government to a fowl's egg, he observed "we shall sooner have the fowl by hatching the egg than by smashing it." On April 14, 1865, at a cabinet meeting, he again urged that Southerners be treated leniently. That night, at Ford's Theater, John Wilkes Booth shot Lincoln, who died the next morning. "Now he belongs to the ages," said Secretary of War Edwin Stanton. But from the thousands who lined the tracks to pay homage as Lincoln's funeral train wended its sad way to Illinois, it was apparent that he truly belonged to the people of America. ♣

Lincoln, pictured opposite in 1863, sported the articles above at Ford's Theater on April 14, 1865, the night he was assassinated. The beaver hat and silver-headed ebony cane were customary. He wore the white kid gloves to the theater to please his wife.

Lincoln joked that the newsboys who sold this picture of the tousled president to the public offered it with the proviso: "Here's your likeness of Old Abe. Will look a good deal better when gets his hair combed."

At right, Lincoln and outgoing President Buchanan ride a carriage to Lincoln's 1861 inauguration, hailed by the postal cover below.

In this composite portrait, Robert Todd Lincoln stands by while his father reads to younger brother Tad. Mary Todd Lincoln looks on with little Willie at her feet. Lincoln used the eyeglasses at right for reading.

Lincoln faces General McClellan *(sixth from left)* near Antietam in October 1862. A month later, Lincoln relieved McClellan of command.

Lincoln penned the Gettysburg Address *(above)* before delivering the speech there in November 1863. His call for the living to complete the "great task" that the defenders of the Union died for took on fresh meaning after his assassination, detailed in articles like the one at right.

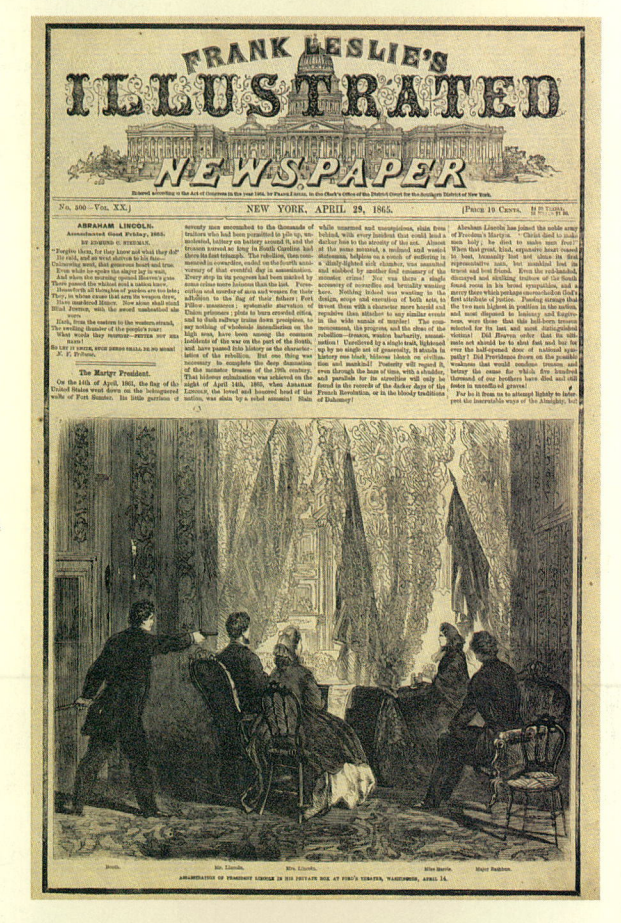

★★★★★★★★★★★
1864
★★★★★★★★★★★

March 9 - General Ulysses S. Grant commissioned lieutenant general. Grant appointed to command armies of the United States.

March 12 - Beginning of the Red River campaign, Louisiana.

April 8 - Battle of Sabine Crossroads (Mansfield), Louisiana. (Red River campaign).

April 9 - Engagement at Pleasant Hill, Louisiana (Red River campaign).

April 12 - Confederates capture Fort Pillow, Tennessee.

April 18-20 Confederate attack on Plymouth, North Carolina, supported by C.S.S. *Albemarle*.

May 4 - Army of the Potomac crosses the Rapidan River in Virginia — start of the Wilderness campaign.

May 5-6 Battle of the Wilderness, Virginia.

May 7 - Federals under William T. Sherman begin Atlanta campaign.

May 8-12 Battle of Spotsylvania Court House, Virginia.

May 11 - Battle of Yellow Tavern, Virginia. Jeb Stuart mortally wounded.

May 12 - Confederates evacuate Dalton, Georgia.

May 14 - Battle of Resaca, Georgia.

65

Phoebe Pember

PHOEBE YATES LEVY PEMBER
1823-1913

During the Civil War, the terrible destruction wrought by modern cannon and minié ball was amplified by the primitive state of medical care. Battle casualties who survived the perfunctory treatment of field surgeons faced a perilous future in the crowded military hospitals of the day. Limbs amputated with unwashed scalpels and saws, or wounds stitched up with dirty needles, inevitably became infected. Infections turned into gangrene, which in turn was worsened by treatment with corrosive chemicals such as turpentine or chlorine—or further amputation. It was little wonder that so many patients who entered hospitals healthy but for their wounds soon sickened and died without apparent cause—as was vividly recorded in *A Southern Woman's Story*, the war memoirs of a Confederate hospital matron named Phoebe Pember.

In 1862, the vivacious 39-year-old Mrs. Pember, a widow from Savannah, Georgia, was placed in charge of housekeeping and patient diet in one of the five divisions of Richmond's Chimborazo Hospital. Chimborazo was then the largest military hospital in the world—treating some 76,000 patients over the course of the war.

Phoebe Pember's appointment as one of the hospital's chief administrators faced vociferous opposition, for it was a job that until then had been reserved for males. And she magnified that resentment by her strict adherence to military regulations regarding the dispensation of neat whiskey—so freely prescribed for its presumed medicinal value that drunkenness was rampant among both patients and doctors. In one case, an inebriated surgeon operating on a soldier with a crushed ankle set the good leg instead of the broken one. The young man died of ensuing complications in one of the many instances of medical ineptness witnessed by the tart Mrs. Pember. Despite her efforts, she often lost her battles to control the supply of alcohol—one of the few anesthetics of the era—but her brisk good sense and resourcefulness in feeding and nursing the more than 15,000 men under her direct care earned her the respect and devotion of many.

Phoebe Pember stayed at her post through the Confederate evacuation of Richmond and its occupation by Union troops in April 1865. She left the hospital, she later reported, with nothing but "a box full of Confederate money and a silver ten cent piece" to see her back to Georgia. She spent the rest of her days in quiet obscurity relieved only by the publication in 1879 of her book—a spritely testament to the vagaries of mid-19th-century hospital life. ♣

The clock that hung on the wall of Chimborazo General Hospital likely chimed out a rigid schedule. Opposite: Daughter of a cultured and wealthy Jewish family from South Carolina, Phoebe Pember faced grueling work as Chimborazo's first matron.

Sprawling on a bluff near Richmond, Chimborazo Hospital suffered from a shortage of medical personnel and the scarcity of supplies. Even so, its mortality rate was a low 10 percent—a statistic improved upon only some 80 years later.

Of Dr. James B. McCaw, Chimborazo's surgeon in chief, Pember wrote, "Wisely he decided to have an educated and efficient woman at the head of his hospital, and having succeeded, never allowed himself to forget that fact."

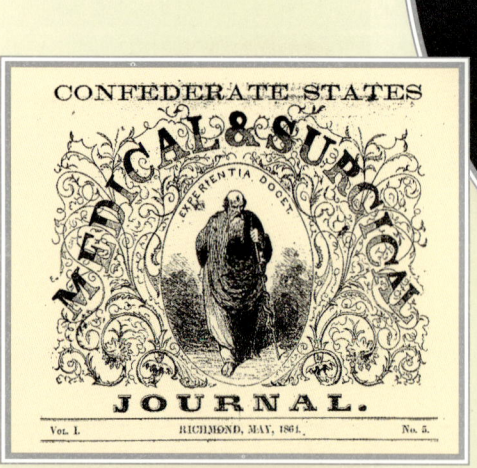

A map drawn in 1862 shows Chimborazo to be a sprawling complex of one-story wards. Later the facilities were enlarged to accommodate as many as 10,000 patients.

The isolated medical community of the Confederacy established its own professional journal, the one above dated May 1864.

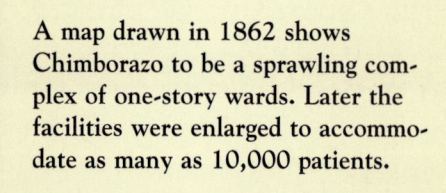

A nurse's apron was a Chimborazo essential.

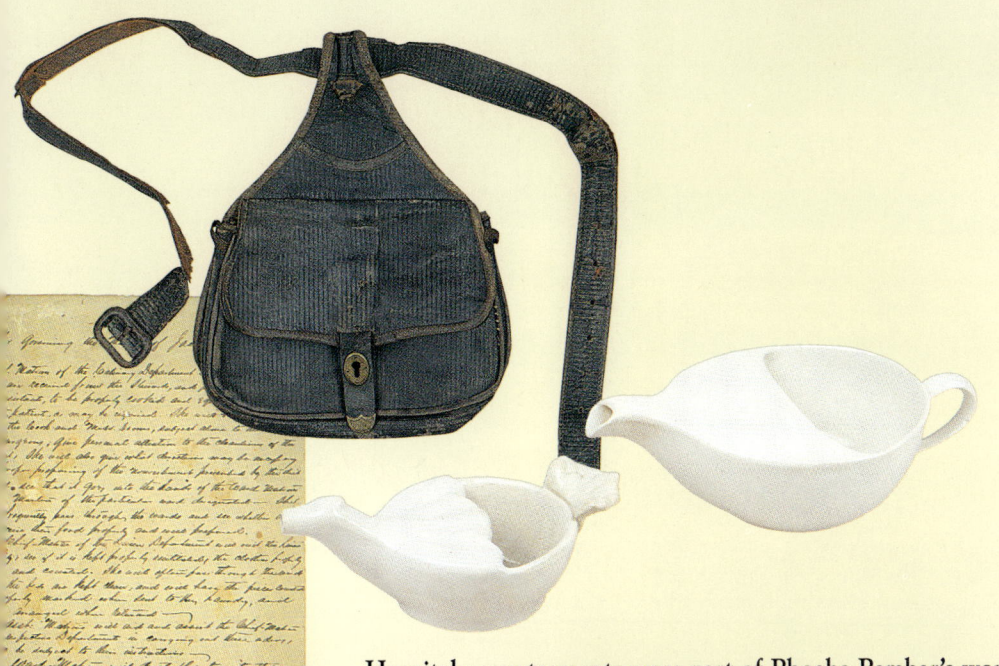

Hospital accoutrements were part of Phoebe Pember's world at Chimborazo: feeding cups, a reticule worn around the waist for carrying supplies, and rules by which to live and work.

As Richmond burns, a cavalry-led group of Confederate officials flees the fallen city. Pember, who stayed at her post, wrote, "No one slept during that night of horror."

Pember's letters to friends, as well as her autobiography, painted a picture of life in wartime Richmond.

69

★★★★★★★★★★★★★★
1 8 6 4
★★★★★★★★★★★★★★

May 15 - Battle of New Market Virginia. Battle of Resaca continues.

May 16 - Battle of Drewry's Bluff (Fort Darling), Virginia.

May 18-19 Fighting renewed at Spotsylvania Court House, Virginia.

May 23-26 Battle of North Anna River, Virginia.

May 25- Operations begin around New Hope Church, Georgia.

June 1-3 Battle of Cold Harbor, Virginia.

June 8 - Lincoln nominated for a second term.

June 14 - Army of the Potomac crosses the James River, Virginia. Battle of Pine Mountain, Georgia.

June 16-18 First Federal assaults on Petersburg, Virginia. Beginning of siege of Petersburg.

June 19 - U.S.S. *Kearsarge* sinks C.S.S. *Alabama* off Cherbourg, France.

June 23 - Engagement at Weldon Railroad, Virginia.

June 27 - Battle of Kennesaw Mountain, Georgia.

July 8 - Reconstruction Proclamation.

July 9 - Battle of Monocacy, Maryland. Early's raid on Washington, D.C.

July 11 - Confederates in Washington suburbs. Fighting at Fort Stevens.

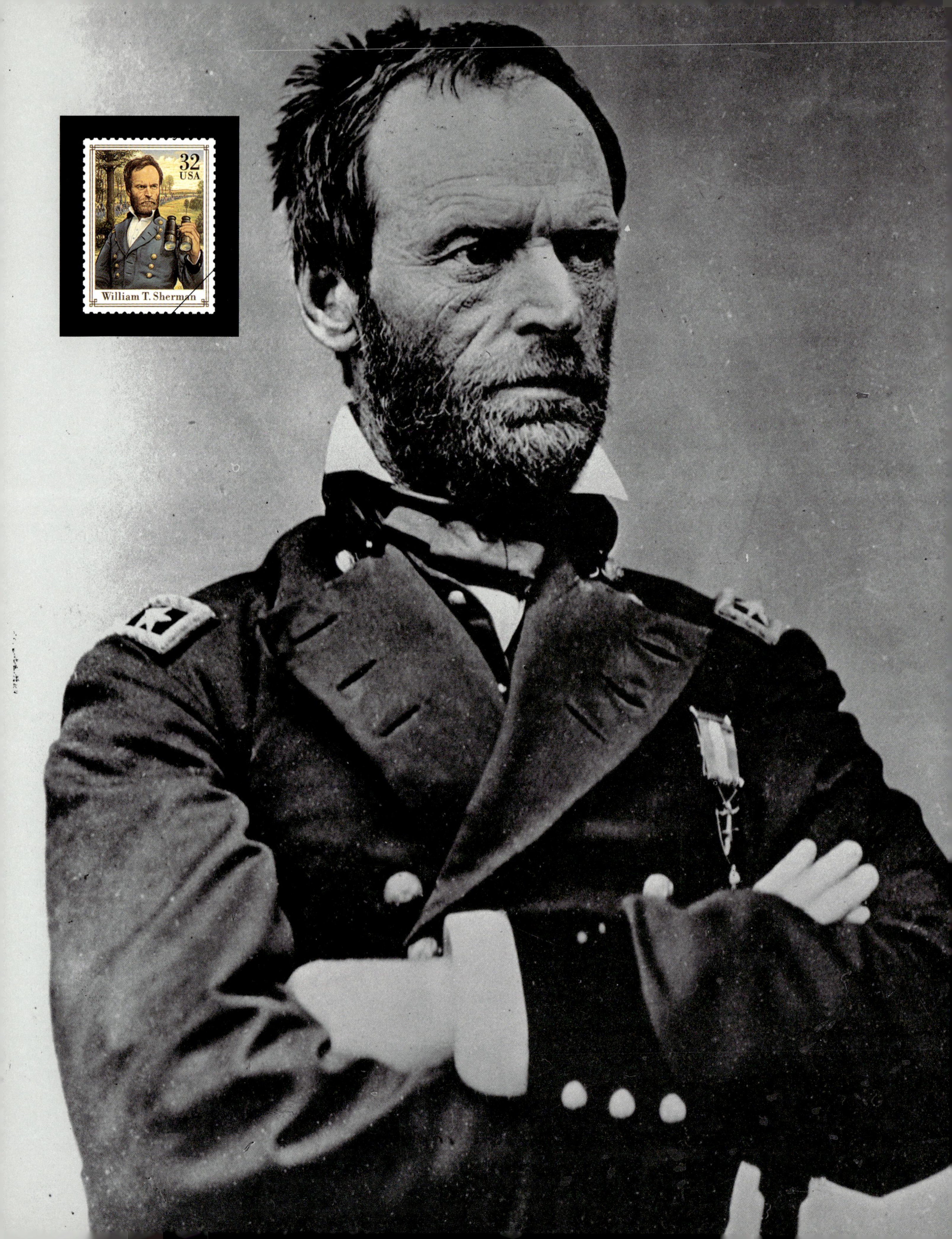
32
USA
William T. Sherman

WILLIAM TECUMSEH SHERMAN
1820-1891

At the outset of hostilities, both North and South expected the Civil War to be fought according to almost knightly codes of honor that excluded the civilian population from the conflict. But as the terrible struggle raged on, and casualties mounted, a new and grimmer style of warfare evolved. In an effort to cripple the Confederacy's ability to feed and supply its armies in the field, Union commanders began to confiscate or destroy Southern crops and livestock. Barns, mills and factories were put to the torch, and thousands of noncombatants left destitute. Union major general William Tecumseh Sherman was a proponent and practitioner of this concept of "total war." Northerners saw him as an avenging angel; to Southerners, he seemed nothing less than the devil himself.

A West Point graduate, Sherman was 41 when the war began, and a civilian. After failing as a banker, he had tried his hand at law, then became superintendent of a military school in Louisiana. Volunteering for the Union, he took command of a brigade and led those troops in the first battle of the war at Bull Run. At Shiloh in April 1862, he served as a division commander in the army of U.S. Grant, who became his staunch ally. Lean, grizzled and indifferent to his personal appearance, Sherman was a soldier's soldier. His troops were mostly tough midwesterners, and they admired the intense, willful commander they called "Cump" or "Uncle Billy." Sherman had his share of battlefield failures in the first part of the war, and came so close to nervous collapse that some newspapers reported he was insane. But by the summer of 1863, when he served as Grant's second-in-command during the Vicksburg campaign, Sherman had made a name as one of the Union's brightest, most energetic and successful leaders. He and Grant were devoted friends. "He stood by me when I was crazy," Sherman once said, "and I stood by him when he was a drunk; and now we stand by each other always."

When Grant was ordered to the eastern theater, Sherman took charge of all Union troops in the West, and in May of 1864 began a campaign to capture Atlanta. By September the city had fallen to the Yankees, and two months later Sherman and more than 60,000 Union soldiers began their infamous march to the sea. Across Georgia to Savannah, then north through the Carolinas, Sherman put his concept of total war into practice, leaving a grim swath of destruction in his wake. The march hastened the end of the war, but left a legacy of bitterness in the minds of many Southerners. Sherman continued to serve in the U.S. Army after the war, and at his retirement in 1884 was general in chief. At his death in 1891 he was widely regarded by Northerners as second only to Grant in his genius for waging war. ♣

As Sherman cut a swath through the South, he destroyed anything that could be of use to the Confederates, including railroads. His troops uprooted rails, heated them over fires, and then twisted them, like the section shown above.

Seated in front of a map of the South, Sherman clasps his son, Thomas Ewing Sherman, known as Tommy. Sherman did not want his boys to become soldiers; he thought a military career was "too full of blind chances."

Sherman's wife, Ellen, a devout Catholic, bore him eight children. His failure to settle down and embrace her faith put a severe strain on their marriage.

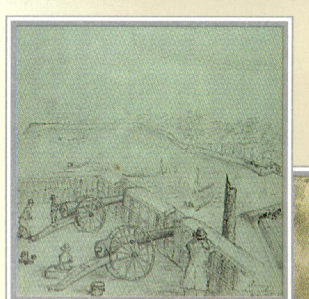

General Sherman *(center, on horseback)*, accompanied by an officer using field glasses, consults the commander of an artillery battery during a bombardment of Atlanta.

Sherman frequently wrote letters to his children, often enclosing souvenirs and sketches of places he and his troops had been. Above left is his drawing of the officers' mess tent near Vicksburg; at right a scene of Federal guns.

General Sherman leans against the breech of a 20-pound Parrott rifle at a Union fort in Atlanta during the Federal occupation of the city.

Henry C. Work's popular patriotic song, "Marching through Georgia," was filled with images that glorified Sherman's men and the Union cause.

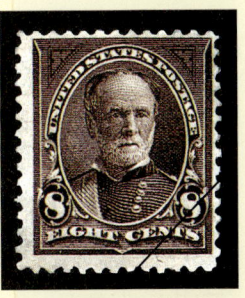

This stamp commemorating Sherman was issued in 1894.

★★★★★★★★★★★★
1864
★★★★★★★★★★★★

July 14 - Battle of Tupelo (Harrisburg), Mississippi.

July 17 - General Joseph E. Johnston replaced by Major General John Bell Hood to command of Army of Tennessee.

July 20 - Battle of Peachtree Creek, Georgia.

July 22 - Battle of Atlanta, Georgia.

July 24 - Second battle of Kernstown, Virginia.

July 28 - Battle of Ezra Church, Georgia.

July 30 - Explosion of the Petersburg Mine (Battle of the Crater). Capture and burning of Chambersburg, Pennsylvania, by Confederates.

August 5 - Battle of Mobile Bay, Alabama.

August 7 - Surrender of Fort Gaines in Mobile Bay, Alabama.

August 18 - Change in Federal policy ends exchange of prisoners.

August 18-19 Battle of Weldon Railroad, Virginia.

August 25 - Battle of Ream's Station, Virginia.

August 31 - James B. McClellan nominated for president on the Democratic ticket. Battle of Jonesborough, Georgia.

September 1 - Confederate forces evacuate Atlanta defenses. Continued fighting at Jonesborough, Georgia.

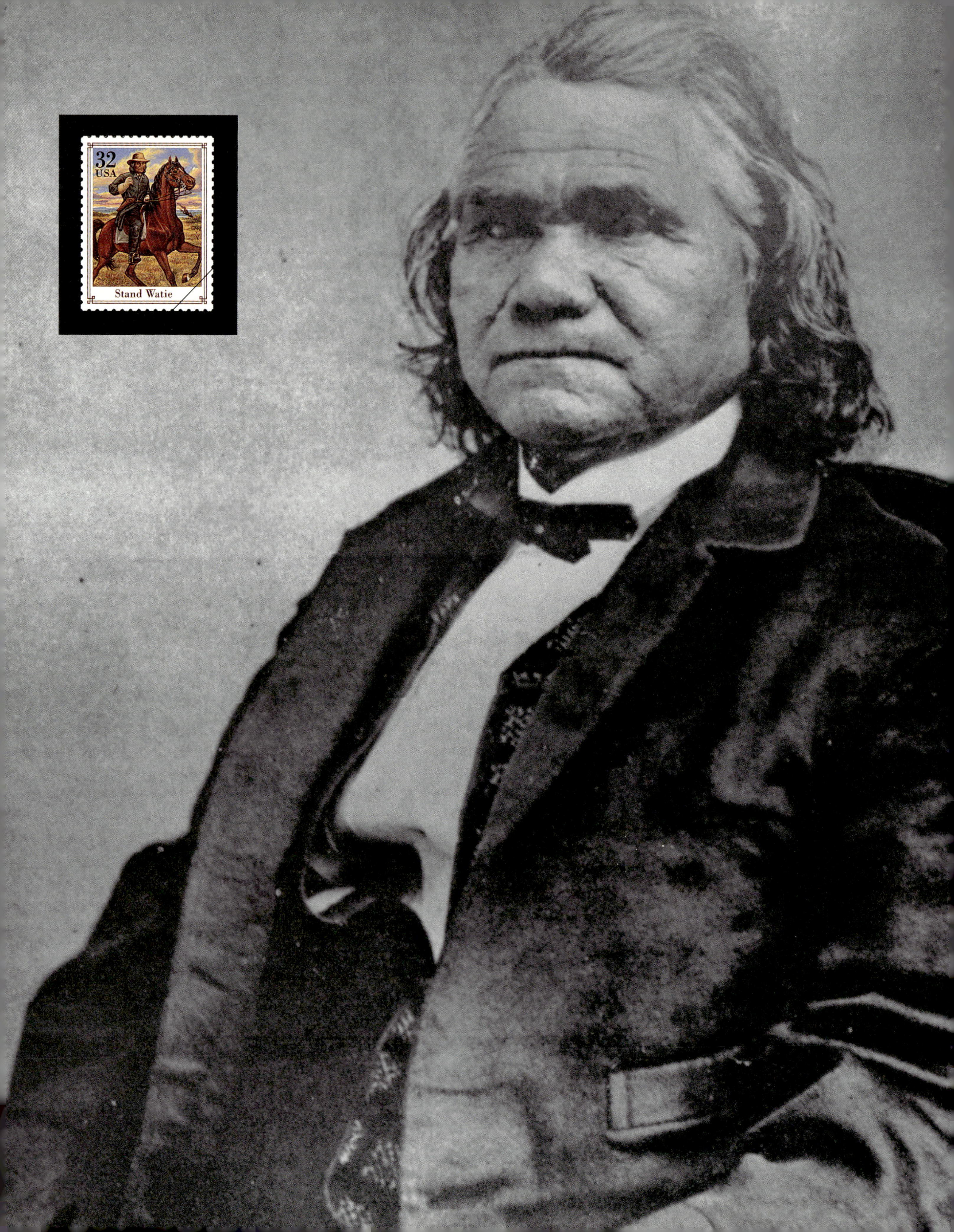
32
USA
Stand Watie

STAND WATIE
(DE-GA-DO-GA)
1806-1871

The highest-ranking Native American to serve in the Civil War, Confederate brigadier general Stand Watie was among the last commanders to lay down his arms—on June 23, 1865, more than two months after Lee's surrender at Appomattox. By then, the Cherokee general was renowned for his bold raids on Federals in the disputed Indian Territory and surrounding states. "I wish I had as much energy in some of my white commanders as he displays," remarked his superior, General Samuel B. Maxey. For Watie as for other embattled Cherokees, however, no laurels could soothe the deep wounds they suffered as a people during the war.

Born on Cherokee land in Georgia, Watie took his first name from a tribal title meaning "stand firm." Schooled by missionaries, he grew familiar with the language and culture of white Southerners yet remained proud of his heritage. Passage of the Indian Removal Act in 1830 drove a wedge through the Cherokee nation. Watie sided with a minority that saw removal west of the Mississippi as inevitable and signed a treaty to that effect in 1835. Most Cherokees spurned the treaty and were ousted by troops. Their bitter journey to the Indian Territory, known as the Trail of Tears, heightened antagonism toward the protreaty leaders, several of whom were put to death—a fate Watie barely escaped.

Tribal divisions resurfaced with the outbreak of the Civil War. As one of a number of Cherokees who were prospering as planters and slaveowners, Watie helped bring about an alliance with the Confederacy, against the wishes of Cherokees who disdained slavery and favored the Union. Commissioned a colonel in July 1861, Watie raised a regiment called the Cherokee Mounted Volunteers that saw action in Arkansas at Pea Ridge in 1862. In 1863, after Unionist Cherokees took control of the tribal capital of Tahlequah, Watie's raiders torched the council house there. He won command of a brigade in 1864, and his men scored many a coup behind enemy lines, including capture of a Federal supply vessel loaded with 16,000 pounds of bacon.

Watie's raiders were chronically undersupplied and often had to make do with what they took from the enemy. Watie himself once claimed a Union greatcoat that was too large for his short frame. As he sat outside his tent one night, a passing soldier spied only the greatcoat in the gloom and tried to make off with it. "Hold on!" Watie snapped. "There's a man in this coat!" After the war, resentments lingered between Watie and his tribal opponents. But few would deny that Stand Watie was a true and tested Cherokee warrior, deserving of their respect. ♣

This Bowie-style knife was carried during the war by Stand Watie, the last Confederate general to surrender. The Cherokee commander bequeathed the knife to his nephew, Will Watie Wheeler, who enlisted under his uncle in 1862, at the age of 15.

Stand Watie *(above)* married Sarah Caroline Bell *(right)* on September 18, 1842.

This battle flag was carried by the 1st Cherokee Mounted Rifles, one of the regiments Watie commanded. The five red stars inside the ring of 11 white ones represent the Indian Territory's five "Civilized Tribes"—Cherokee, Creek, Chickasaw, Choctaw, and Seminole.

A northern view of Pea Ridge misrepresents Confederate Cherokees as wild Indians in native dress.

The CN on this envelope addressed to Stand Watie refers to the Cherokee Nation.

76

Albert Pike *(left)*, a 300-pound Arkansas planter who knew several Indian languages, negotiated the Confederate-Cherokee alliance that Stand Watie and his recruits embraced and other Cherokees opposed.

At war's end, peace talks in Washington, D.C., drew these Cherokee delegates, including Stand Watie's son, Saladin Ridge Watie *(second from left)*. Stand Watie had returned home when this picture was taken, but he and his Confederate subordinates—including Lieutenant Colonel Clement Neeley Vann *(right)*—acknowledged defeat and tried to rebuild their nation.

★★★★★★★★★★★
1864
★★★★★★★★★★★

September 2 - Federal troops enter Atlanta, Georgia.

September 7 - Federal general William T. Sherman orders forced evacuation of Atlanta civilians.

September 19 - Third Battle of Winchester (Opequon Creek), Virginia.

September 23 - Battle of Fisher's Hill, Virginia.

September 29 - October 2 Battle of Peeble's Farm, Virginia. Battle of Fort Harrison (Chaffin's Farm), Virginia.

October 5 - Engagement at Allatoona, Georgia.

October 7 - Commerce raider C.S.S. *Florida* captured by U.S.S. *Wachusett* in Bahia Harbor, Brazil.

October 9 - Engagement at Tom's Brook, Virginia.

October 19 - Battle of Cedar Creek (Belle Grove), Virginia. Confederates raid Saint Albans, Vermont.

October 23 - Battle of Westport, Missouri.

October 27 - Engagement at Burgess' Mill (Boydton Plank Road), Virginia. C.S.S. *Albemarle* sunk at Plymouth, North Carolina.

November 8 - Abraham Lincoln reelected president of the United States.

November 16 - Sherman begins march to the sea.

32 USA

David Farragut

DAVID GLASGOW FARRAGUT
1801-1870

A supremely confident commander, Admiral David Farragut inspired the Union with his decisiveness and daring. In the opinion of Secretary of the Navy Gideon Welles, he would "more willingly take great risks to obtain great results than any officer in either army or navy."

Farragut entered the war with a half-century of naval experience, having taken to sea as a midshipman at the age of 10 under his guardian, Commander David Porter. Intensely ambitious, Farragut rose to the rank of commander himself in 1841 and sought glory in the Mexican War, only to be relegated to routine blockade duty. In 1861, opposing secession, he left his home in Norfolk, Virginia, for New York. There, he at first received only a minor assignment from a Union navy wary of Southerners. But in early 1862, he was given command of a squadron with orders to storm the Confederate forts astride the mouth of the Mississippi River and take New Orleans. He opened the attack by shelling the two strongholds from safe positions. When the barrage failed, he chose to run the gauntlet. He had been awaiting this command all his life, he wrote to his wife beforehand, and needed a victory "to complete the scene." In just two hours, at a cost of a single Union warship, his fleet blasted past the forts and crushed a Confederate flotilla below New Orleans. Federal troops occupied the city unopposed.

In the jubilant aftermath, Farragut was promoted to become the navy's only admiral. After operating along the Mississippi in 1863, he set his sights on Mobile Bay, the Confederacy's last important outlet to the Gulf of Mexico. Attacking on August 5, 1864, Farragut's fleet had to thread a channel barely 200 yards wide, flanked on one side by a fort with 47 guns and on the other side by shallows laced with torpedoes, or submerged mines. The advance faltered when an ironclad in the lead struck a mine and sank. Observing from his flagship *Hartford*, Farragut decided to skirt the stalled ships and brave the minefield. He issued a command that became legend: "Damn the torpedoes! Full speed ahead!" The *Hartford* grazed several mines without detonating them, and Farragut's initiative succeeded in breaking the logjam. As his fleet entered the bay, the Confederate ironclad *Tennessee* challenged the *Hartford* and dueled with her at close quarters before other Union warships weighed in and disabled the ironclad.

The taking of Mobile Bay crowned Farragut's career. It also strengthened the Union strategically and cheered a public hungry for bold leadership. As Farragut summed up his approach to battle: "I will attack regardless of consequences, and never turn back." ♣

Farragut stood for the portrait at left following his promotion to rear admiral. Above is the ship's bell from Farragut's flagship the U.S.S. *Hartford*.

"Don't flinch from that fire, boys. There's a hotter fire than that for those who don't do their duty."

Captain David Glasgow Farragut, U.S.N.

Lieutenant Farragut, commanding officer of the sloop *Erie* in 1838

Running the Confederate gauntlet at the mouth of the Mississippi on April 25, 1862, Farragut's flagship *Hartford* (left) trades shots with the Confederate ram *Manassas* and heads for New Orleans.

Farragut's presentation sword and sheath

The deck of the *Hartford* seethes with action as the Federal flagship unleashes a full broadside on the Confederate ironclad *Tennessee* in Mobile Bay on August 5, 1864. Admiral Farragut stands calmly in the rigging while a gun crew in the foreground rushes to reload a smoking cannon.

Confederate torpedo from Mobile Bay

1864

November 21 - Confederate Army of Tennessee advances toward Tennessee.

November 30 - Battle of Franklin, Tennessee.

December 13 - Capture of Fort McAllister near Savannah, Georgia.

December 15-16 Battle of Nashville, Tennessee.

December 20 - Confederates evacuate Savannah, Georgia.

December 24-25 First Federal assault on Fort Fisher at Wilmington, North Carolina.

1865

January 13-15 Assault and capture of Fort Fisher, Wilmington, North Carolina.

January 19 - Sherman begins march from Savannah to Carolinas.

January 24 - Prisoner exchange to resume.

January 31 - U.S. House of Representatives passes amendment abolishing slavery. Robert E. Lee named general in chief of Confederate armies.

February 3 - Conference at Hampton Roads between Confederate envoys and Lincoln and Seward.

February 5-7 Battle of Hatcher's Run, Virginia.

February 17 - Federals capture and burn Columbia, South Carolina. Confederates evacuate Charleston, South Carolina.

Mary Chesnut

Mary Boykin Miller Chesnut
1823-1886

"It was a way I had, always, to stumble in on the real show," reflected Southerner Mary Chesnut, the Civil War's most famous diarist, 20 years after the conflict ended. Indeed, few chroniclers were so perfectly placed to document the drama of the Confederacy's brief life and cataclysmic demise as this sharply observant and cultured plantation aristocrat. The daughter of a former governor of South Carolina, Mary Boykin Miller was born into the tightly interwoven and insular social circle that produced most of the South's prominent military and civil leaders.

She was married at 17 to James Chesnut, a wealthy Princeton-educated lawyer and son of one of the state's largest landowners. Elected to the United States Senate in 1858, Chesnut abruptly resigned his seat upon Lincoln's election two years later and went on to serve the Confederacy as a congressman, Army staff officer, and aide to President Jefferson Davis. At her husband's side in Washington, Richmond, Charleston and Montgomery, Mary Chesnut, an inveterate hostess who entertained constantly despite wartime privations, was at the vortex of Southern politics and society.

Chesnut began her diary in February 1861, the month South Carolina seceded from the Union. A talented writer who had received a rigorous classical education, she approached her task with the scrupulous eye of a historian, conscious that her unique perspective as a witness might "at some future day afford facts about these times and prove useful to more important people." Over the course of the war, she filled 50 copybooks with compelling accounts of domestic and public events and deft sketches of such Southern heroes as Stonewall Jackson ("a one idea man") and Robert E. Lee ("so cold and quiet and grand").

Although staunchly loyal to the South, Chesnut refused to romanticize her region, deploring above all the institution of slavery, which she depicted in brutally candid terms and pronounced "monstrous." She closed her diary on August 2, 1865, and from then until her death in 1886 worked to edit the 400,000-word manuscript into publishable form. A much shortened version was brought out by her literary heirs in 1905, as *A Diary from Dixie*. Today, historians regard the subsequent, more complete edition originally published in 1949 as one of the finest literary works of its time and treasure its vivid picture of the South in wartime as a rich source of detail and insight. ♣

This feather fan was a gift to Mary Chesnut from President Jefferson Davis on Christmas Day, 1863. The two families remained lifelong friends. Opposite, in a previously unpublished tintype, Mary and her husband James pose in the year of their wedding, 1840.

Mary Chesnut was 33 when she sat for this portrait. Her well-known wit and charm prompted one gentleman to remark, "The most comfortable chair is beside Mrs. Chesnut."

As the emissary of Jefferson Davis, James Chesnut, Jr., rowed to Union-occupied Fort Sumter to demand its surrender. When refused, he relayed the order that the fort be fired upon.

Jubilant Richmonders gather at the capitol to celebrate the victory at Manassas in July 1861. On the night the news arrived, Chesnut wrote, "Times were too wild with excitement to stay in bed."

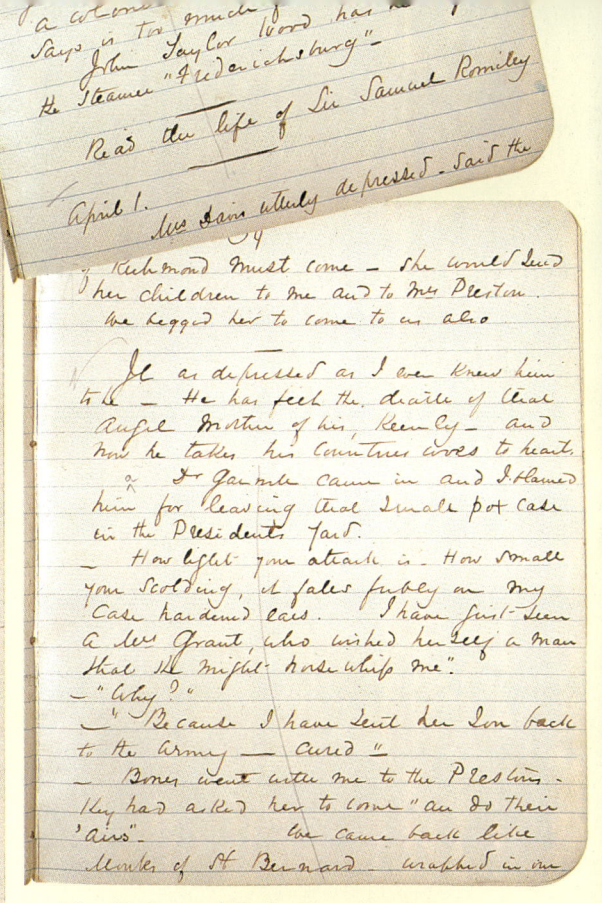

The Richmond *Daily Examiner* announcement of a theater performance and a minstrel show in January of 1864 *(left)* hints at the forced gaiety that pervaded the capitol. But defeat was in the air; in April of that year, Chesnut wrote in her diary of the despair *(above)*.

Mary Chesnut's lap desk, its exterior inlaid with mother-of-pearl and interior of gold-embossed leather, was her constant companion throughout the war.

1865

February 22 - Capture of Wilmington, North Carolina. Joseph E. Johnston restored to command Army of Tennessee.

March 2 - Engagement at Waynesboro, Virginia.

March 4 - Inauguration of Lincoln.

March 8-10 Battle of Kinston, North Carolina.

March 11 - Federal troops capture Fayetteville, North Carolina.

March 16 - Battle of Averasborough, North Carolina.

March 19-21 Battle of Bentonville, North Carolina.

March 25 - Confederate assault on Fort Steadman, Petersburg, Virginia. Siege of Mobile, Alabama, begins.

April 1 - Battle of Five Forks, Virginia.

April 2 - Confederate government evacuates Richmond, Virginia. Federal troops capture portions of the Petersburg lines. Selma, Alabama, captured by Federals.

April 3 - Federal troops enter Richmond and Petersburg, Virginia.

April 4 - Lincoln visits Richmond.

April 6 - Battle of Sayler's Creek, Virginia.

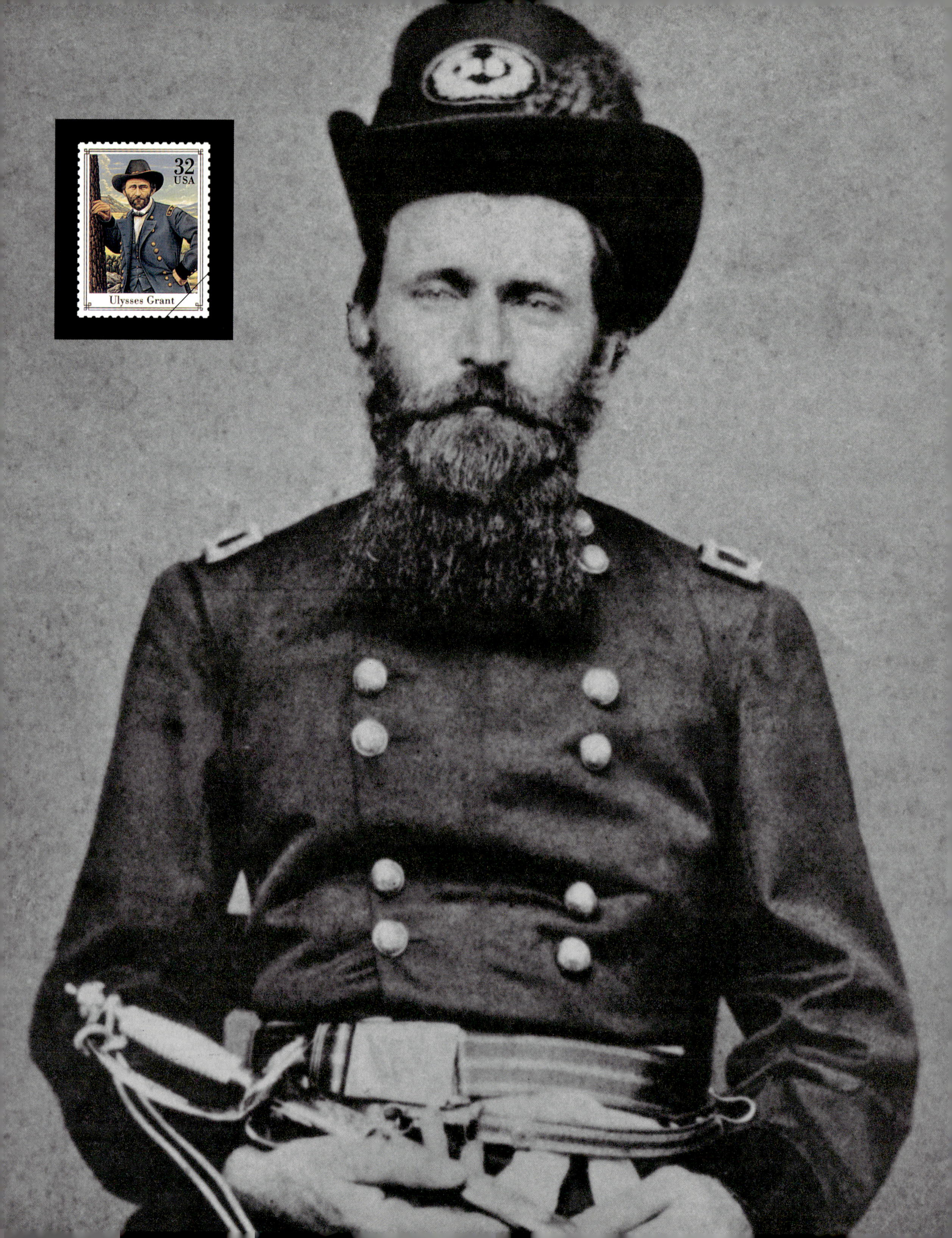
32
USA
Ulysses Grant

ULYSSES S. GRANT
1822-1885

Had it not been for the Civil War, Ulysses Simpson Grant probably would have lived out his life in obscurity. There was little in his makeup to indicate he would become the Union's most famous soldier. An Ohio native, he graduated from West Point in 1843, but with an undistinguished record. Although he served bravely in the Mexican War, he resigned from the army in 1854—some said to avoid a court-martial for drunkenness. For nearly seven years prior to the Civil War, U.S. Grant moved aimlessly from job to job—farming, clerking, dabbling in real estate, and even selling firewood. When war broke out in 1861 he was working in the family leather-goods store at Galena, Illinois.

As a new volunteer officer, however, Grant revealed impressive assets: intelligence, a flair for leadership, and a taste for fighting. In the closing months of 1861, Grant had been promoted to the rank of brigadier general and was beginning to display his talent for waging grim, determined war. His seizure of Confederate Forts Henry and Donelson, which capitulated to his demand of "unconditional surrender," and his victory at Shiloh made the quiet, unassuming general a national hero. In July 1863, Grant's dog-ged and brilliant campaigning brought about the surrender of the Mississippi River fortress of Vicksburg. Later that year he soundly defeated Braxton Bragg's Confederate army at Chattanooga—a victory that persuaded President Lincoln to appoint Grant general in chief of all Union armies in the field. His greatest virtues, according to his good friend William T. Sherman, were "simplicity of character, singleness of purpose."

Early in 1864, Grant traveled east to direct the Army of the Potomac in yet another effort to defeat Robert E. Lee's Army of Northern Virginia. At first glance the eastern soldiers found little inspiring about the nondescript man garbed in a plain uniform, who always seemed to be chewing on a cigar. But once Grant joined battle with Lee at the Wilderness in May 1864, the troops began to realize just how gritty and determined their commander was. In a month of terrible fighting Grant's forces lost more than 50,000 men, but succeeded in pushing Lee ever southward, to the defenses of Richmond.

Following a nine-month siege of Lee's army at Petersburg, the depleted Southern ranks were at last brought to bay at Appomattox Court House, and Grant accepted Lee's surrender on April 9, 1865. In the postwar years, Grant's fame as the Union's preeminent soldier brought him two terms as president. Although his tenure was marked by scandal and mismanagement, few Northerners ever doubted the integrity of the humble man who rose to greatness when his country called. ♣

In March 1864, Congress honored Grant with this unique gold medal. As one officer described it, the award "was three pounds in weight, on one side a bad likeness of Grant; on the reverse a goddess in an impossible position." Opposite, Brigadier General Grant wears a new dress uniform in a photo taken in October 1861.

BOGGS & GRANT,
GENERAL AGENTS,
COLLECT RENTS, NEGOTIATE LOANS, BUY AND SELL REAL ESTATE, ETC., ETC.
NO. 35 PINE STREET,
Between Second and Third,
SAINT LOUIS, MO.

Toward the end of the war, Grant and his wife, Julia, sit for a family portrait with their children *(from left)*, Nellie, Jesse, Fred and Ulysses Jr. Inset is Grant's business card for a real estate partnership formed in 1859.

Grant was a 27-year-old infantry quartermaster at Sackets Harbor, New York, when this daguerreotype was taken in 1849. Recently married, he lived with his bride, Julia, in cramped quarters.

Grant, on horseback *(center)*, watches his troops advance on Fort Donelson in Tennessee. Two black servants carry a wounded Federal officer *(right)* to an impromptu field hospital behind an artillery battery *(left)*.

88

Grant writes a message while seated on a log in Virginia's Wilderness in the spring of 1864. In that season he embarked on a campaign to capture Richmond and defeat the Confederacy once and for all.

Grant earned the shoulder boards of a full general in 1866.

More concerned with comfort than appearance, Grant is shown wearing his general's uniform with his usual casual air.

Grant meets with General Sherman, President Lincoln and Admiral David D. Porter to discuss strategy and peace terms aboard the steamer *River Queen* at City Point, Virginia, in late March of 1865.

Grant's presentation sword

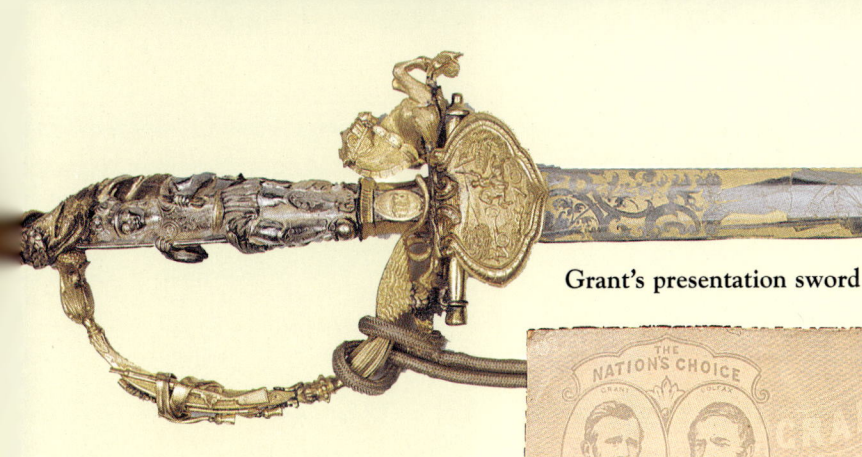

This postal cover touts the Republican ticket for 1868: Grant for president with Schuyler Colfax of Indiana as his running mate.

A political cartoon portrays a beaming Uncle Sam congratulating President Grant on his landslide re election in 1872. His opponent, Horace Greeley, is shown falling into a political purgatory populated by squabbling allies.

A photograph taken on July 22, 1885, shows Grant on the porch of his cottage at Mount McGregor, New York. Dying of throat cancer, he had recently finished the difficult task of writing his memoirs.

This Grant stamp was issued in 1890.

★★★★★★★★★★★
1 8 6 5
★★★★★★★★★★★

April 9 - Surrender of the Army of Northern Virginia at Appomattox Court House, Virginia.

April 12 - Surrender of Mobile, Alabama.

April 14 - Lincoln assassinated at Ford's Theater in Washington, D.C. Federal flag raised over Fort Sumter, South Carolina.

April 15 - Death of Lincoln. Andrew Johnson takes oath of office as president of the United States.

April 26 - Surrender of the Army of Tennessee by General Johnson near Durham, North Carolina.

May 4 - Surrender of Confederate forces under General Richard Taylor at Citronelle, Alabama.

May 10 - President Jefferson Davis captured near Irwinville, Georgia.

May 12 - Engagement at Palmito Ranch, near Brownsville, Texas.

May 23 - Grand Review of the Army of the Potomac in Washington, D.C.

May 24 - Grand Review of Sherman's Army in Washington, D.C.

May 26 - Surrender of the Confederate Army of Trans-Mississippi at New Orleans, Louisiana.

32 USA

The Story Behind the Stamps

Postage stamps have long paid tribute to decisive events in the nation's history and to the men and women who met great challenges. No crisis ever demanded more of the American people and their leaders than the Civil War. And no single image could hope to convey the sweep of that struggle. To commemorate the conflict, the Postal Service commissioned this series—the latest in its Classic Collections of 20 related stamps on one sheet. Featured here are four battles and 16 notable figures, embodying many facets of the War between the States.

Assembling this collection involved two delicate tasks. First, the roster of important Civil War battles and leaders would have to be winnowed down from several dozen worthy candidates to a score. Then, each subject would have to be captured in an image that was both striking and historically accurate. Fulfilling those tasks took the concerted effort of more than a dozen individuals, working over 14 months.

The Postal Service began the selection process by consulting four experts on the Civil War: Edwin C. Bearss, former Chief Historian of the National Park Service; Howard J. Coffin, an authority on Civil War battlefields; Dr. William J. Cooper, Jr., Professor of History at Louisiana State University; and Dr. James M. MacPherson, Edwards Professor of American History at Princeton University and the Pulitzer Prize-winning author of *Battle Cry of Freedom*. Each was asked to compile a list of individuals and battles that they considered to be most significant in the course of the war. When the four lists were condensed into one, nearly 60 finalists remained. That list was then narrowed down by the consultants with the assistance of noted historian Shelby Foote, author of the three-volume history, *The Civil War: A Narrative*.

The final roster, arrived at after much discussion, was well balanced. Eight of the individuals selected were associated with the Union and eight with the Confederacy. Some leading commanders on both sides had to be omitted. But the selection conveyed

Mark Hess, Illustrator

the breadth of the conflict by including prominent men and women behind the lines whose words and deeds helped define the struggle.

Once the subjects had been selected, attention shifted to the problem of how best to portray them. The accomplished artist Mark Hess began his work on the collection by studying many existing photographs and paintings of his subjects before drawing up sketches. Certain images had become etched in the imagination of the public, and Hess chose to incorporate them—General Lee with his horse Traveller, General Grant leaning against a tree. But as the consultants studied the artist's preliminary sketches, questions arose. Should Lee be depicted in his field uniform, which displayed only his colonel's stars, or should Hess follow artistic convention and portray Lee in a dress uniform bearing his general's wreath? (In the end, accuracy prevailed and Lee was shown in his field uniform.) Some consultants questioned not only the size and arrangement of the buttons on Major General Winfield Hancock's tunic, but also the spacing. Others wondered what the smoke from the *Monitor* and the *Virginia* would have looked like during their celebrated showdown. Hess spent untold hours sketching and resketching, submitting each successive version for critique.

Questions that stumped even the specialists were tackled by a research firm, PhotoAssist. In the case of the *Monitor* and the *Virginia*, the researchers tracked down logs for the two ironclads in the National Archives, which revealed weather conditions on the day of the engagement—and even specified the type of coal the ships burned (anthracite). Armed with this data, Hess was able to portray the color, quantity, and drift of the smoke with unprecedented accuracy. Many other nagging issues were resolved through painstaking research. Did General Sherman wear a wedding ring? No.

As Hess completed each small painting, he sent it to Washington for a final review by the consultants and by postal officials. Among the critics evaluating each painting was the art director for the Civil War collection, Dick Sheaff, who has coordinated

Christina Shutes *(left)* and Louis Plummer, Researchers

Carl Burcham, Project Manager, U.S.P.S.

the design for numerous stamp projects over the past decade. Sheaff had to consider the effect of reducing each of the 4.75" x 6" canvasses to the size of a postage stamp. Several questions ran through his mind: Would the reduced image be clear and distinct? Was enough of the canvas covered with light tones for the optical scanners of the Postal Service's cancellation equipment to detect the phosphor tagging that marks a stamp as authentic? Were the colors used for all 21 paintings (including the title banner across the top) close enough in range to allow for accurate color reproduction when they were printed together on a single sheet?

Only after Sheaff and the others were fully satisfied did production proceed. The result of all these efforts, from conception to execution, is a Civil War collection that offers the public a faithful portrait of an epic conflict and its defining figures.

Dick Sheaff, Art Director

Citizen's Stamp Advisory Committee *(left to right, front)* Meredith Davis, Dr. Virginia Noelke, Chairman, Dr. Doug Lewis, *(back row)* Phil Meggs, Terrence McCaffrey

Terrence McCaffrey, Stamp Design, U.S.P.S.

SPECIAL THANKS TO
UNITED STATES POSTAL SERVICE

CARL BURCHAM
PROJECT MANAGEMENT

VALOREE VARGO
PROJECT MANAGEMENT

TERRY MCCAFFREY
DESIGN AND QUALITY CONTROL

PEGGY TARTAL
FULFILLMENT AND DISTRIBUTION

ALAN VALSI
PRINTING PROCUREMENT

◆

TIME LIFE BOOKS
IS A DIVISION OF

TIME LIFE INCORPORATED

PRESIDENT AND
CHIEF EXECUTIVE OFFICER
JOHN M. FAHEY

PRESIDENT, TIME-LIFE BOOKS
JOHN D. HALL

TIME LIFE
CUSTOM PUBLISHING

VICE PRESIDENT AND PUBLISHER
TERRY NEWELL

DIRECTOR OF
CUSTOM PUBLISHING
FRANCES C. MANGAN

EDITORIAL DIRECTOR
DONIA ANN STEELE

MANAGER,
SALES AND OPERATIONS
PHYLLIS A. GARDNER

MANAGER,
NEW BUSINESS DEVELOPMENT
REBECCA WHEELER

SENIOR ART DIRECTOR
CHRISTOPHER M. REGISTER

PRODUCTION MANAGER
CAROLYN BOUNDS

QUALITY ASSURANCE MANAGER
JAMES D. KING

ASSOCIATE PROGRAM MANAGER
WENDY BLYTHE

DESIGN
REDRUTH,
ROBIN BRAY, PROPRIETOR

TIME LIFE BOOKS

EDITOR
HENRY WOODHEAD

ADMINISTRATIVE EDITOR
PHILIP BRANDT GEORGE

PICTURE EDITOR
PAULA YORK-SODERLUND

TEXT EDITOR
STEPHEN G. HYSLOP

ASSOCIATE EDITORS
RESEARCH/WRITING
HARRIS J. ANDREWS,
KIRK DENKLER,
GEMMA VILLANUEVA

COPY EDITOR
GREG EDMONDSON

PICTURE COORDINATOR
PAIGE HENKE

EDITORIAL ASSISTANT
CHRISTINE HIGGINS

SPECIAL CONTRIBUTORS
LYDIA PRESTON HICKS, BRIAN C. POHANKA, GERALD P. TYSON (TEXT);
PATRICIA CASSIDY,
RUTH GOLDBERG,
KATHERINE MARGARETHA WEST

CORRESPONDENT
CHRISTINA LIEBERMAN (NEW YORK) VALUABLE ASSISTANCE WAS ALSO PROVIDED BY ELIZABETH BROWN AND DANIEL DONNELLEY (NEW YORK)

PICTURE CREDITS

The sources for the illustrations for this book are listed below. Credits from left to right are separated by semicolons; credits from top to bottom by dashes.

COVER: Valentine Museum, Richmond, Va. **ENDSHEETS:** National Museum of American History, Smithsonian Institution, Washington, DC, photographed by Steven C. Tuttle. **2, 3:** The Western Reserve Historical Society, Cleveland, Ohio. **6:** Library of Congress (LC) No. USZ62-7816. **7:** Courtesy of The Charleston Museum, Charleston, S.C. **8:** Courtesy Louisiana State Museum, photographed by Jackson Hill; National Archives (NA) Neg. No. 111-BA-4687—The Bettmann Archive; (LC) No. 39380. **9:** Frank and Marie-Therese Wood Print Collections, Alexandria, Va.—courtesy Charles L. Blockson, Curator Afro-American Collection, photographed by Larry Sherer; Culver Pictures, Inc.—The Bettmann Archive. **10:** (LC) No. B8184-B4146. **11:** North Carolina Museum of History, Division of Archives and History, Dept. of Cultural Resources, Raleigh, N.C., photographed by Larry Sherer. **12:** Massachusetts Commandery Military Order of the Loyal Legion and the US Army Military History Institute (MASS-MOLLUS/USAMHI), copied by A. Pierce Bounds; inset, The Museum of the Confederacy, Richmond, Va., photographed by Larry Sherer—inset, National Postal Museum, Smithsonian Institution, Washington, DC—painting by John Wood Dodge, National Portrait Gallery, Smithsonian Institution/Art Resource, N.Y.; Beauvior, The Jefferson Davis Shrine, Biloxi, Miss.; painting by John Robertson, The Museum of the Confederacy, photographed by Katherine Wetzel. **13:** The Huntington Library, San Marino, Calif.—(LC) No. B8184-10311—Beauvoir, The Jefferson Davis Shrine, Biloxi, Miss. **14:** Valentine Museum, Richmond, Va. **15:** The Museum of the Confederacy, Richmond, Va., photographed by Larry Sherer. **16:** Painting by Benjamin Franklin Reinhardt, National Portrait Gallery, Smithsonian Institution/Art Resource, N.Y.—from *BATTLES AND LEADERS OF THE CIVIL WAR*, vol. 1, published by the Century Company, 1884-1887—The Museum of the Confederacy, Richmond, Va., photographed by Katherine Wetzel. **17:** The Museum of the Confederacy, Richmond, Va., photographed by Larry Sherer—Eleanor S. Brockenbrough Library/The Museum of the Confederacy, Richmond, Va., photographed by Larry Sherer—(LC) No. B8172-2109. **18:** MASS-MOLLUS/USAMHI, copied by A. Pierce Bounds; inset, The Chrysler Museum, Norfolk, Va., Gift of Anson T. and Philip J. McCook. **19:** Courtesy of the Mariners' Museum, Newport News, Va. **20, 21:** (LC) No. NH 61920—US Naval Historical Center Photograph—courtesy of the Mariners' Museum, Newport News, Va.—US Naval Academy Museum, Annapolis, Md.; The Collection of Jay P. Altmayer, photographed by Larry Cantrell; courtesy of the Mariners' Museum, Newport News, Va.—National Postal Museum, Smithsonian Institution, Washington, DC—The Museum of the Confederacy, Richmond, Va., photographed by Katherine Wetzel—Smithsonian Institution, Washington, DC. **22:** Courtesy of Stonewall Jackson Foundation, Lexington, Virginia. **23:** Stonewall Jackson's Headquarters Museum/Winchester-Frederick County Historical Society, photographed by Larry Sherer—The VMI Museum, Lexington, Va., photographed by Larry Sherer. **24:** Courtesy of Stonewall Jackson Foundation, Lexington, Virginia (2)—courtesy of Stonewall Jackson Foundation, Lexington, Virginia, photographed by Larry Sherer—inset, The Museum of the Confederacy, Richmond, Va., photographed by Larry Sherer. **25:** Courtesy of Stonewall Jackson Foundation, Lexington, Virginia—inset, courtesy Christopher D.W. Nelson—painting by Charles Hoffbauer, courtesy the Virginia Historical Society, Richmond, Va.—Eleanor S. Brockenbrough Library/The Museum of the Confederacy, Richmond, Va., photographed by Larry Sherer. **26:** (LC) No. B818-100426. **27:** Fort St. Joseph Museum, Niles, Mich. **28, 29:** Courtesy Christopher D.W. Nelson; photograph by J.W. Campbell, Chicago Historical Society, Neg. No. ICHi-10484; courtesy Confederate Memorial Hall, New Orleans, photographed by Larry Sherer—Painting by Thure de Thulstrup, The Seventh Regiment Fund, Inc: ,The American Heritage Picture Collection—Gettysburg National Military Park, photographed by Larry Sherer—(NA) Neg. No. 111-BA1172; (LC) No. B8184 1685. **30:** (NA), copied by Evan H. Sheppard. **31:** Courtesy Gettysburg National Military Park, photographed by A. Pierce Bounds. **32, 33:** Brian Pohanka (2)—(NA) Neg. No. 111-B-2022; painting by Julian Scott, courtesy Smithsonian Institution, Washington, DC—from *RECOLLECTIONS OF A PRIVATE: A STORY OF THE ARMY OF THE POTOMAC* by Warren Lee Goss, Thomas Y. Crowell & Co., New York, 1890; Frank and Marie-Thérèse Wood Print Collections, Alexandria, Va. **34:** (NA) Neg. No. 111-B-1857. **35:** (LC), photographed by Evan H. Sheppard. **36:** (LC) No. B815-588; inset, (LC), photographed by Evan H. Sheppard—(LC) No. LCMS-11973-1; Frank and Marie-Thérèse Wood Print Collections, Alexandria, Va.—National Postal Museum, Smithsonian Institution, Washington, DC—courtesy Clara Barton House, Glen Echo, Md., photographed by Evan H. Sheppard. **37:** (LC), No. USZ62-4427; courtesy Clara Barton House, Glen Echo, Md., photographed by Evan H. Sheppard—(LC), photographed by Evan H. Sheppard (5)—(LC) No. USZ6-203. **38:** Painting attributed to W.B. Cox, courtesy the Virginia Historical Society, Richmond, Va. **39:** The Museum of the Confederacy, Richmond, Va., photographed by Katherine Wetzel. **40:** MASS-MOLLUS/USAMHI, copied by A. Pierce Bounds; Washington/Custis/Lee Collection, Washington and Lee University, Lexington, Va.—painting by B.J. Lossing, Arlington House Collection, National Park Service, Arlington, Va., photographed by Larry Sherer. **41:** Drawings by Robert E. Lee, duPont Library, Stratford Hall Plantation, photographed by Larry Sherer—Western Americana Collection, Beinecke Rare Book and Manuscript Library, Yale University, copied by Henry Groskinsky—courtesy D. Mark Katz. **42:** Painting by Charles Hoffbauer, courtesy Virginia Historical Society, Richmond, Va., photographed by Henry Groskinsky—MASS-MOLLUS/USAMHI, copied by A. Pierce Bounds; The Museum of the Confederacy, Richmond, Va., photographed by Larry Sherer. **43:** Virginia Historical Society, Richmond, Va.; inset, US Postal Service—Virginia Historical Society, Richmond, Va. **44:** Painting by Frederick A. Chapman, The Civil War Library and Museum, on loan to Chancellorsville Battlefield Visitor Center. **45:** National Park Service, Fredericksburg and Spotsylvania National Military Park. **46:** From *BATTLES AND LEADERS OF THE CIVIL WAR*, vol. 3, published by the Century Co., New York, 1887—(LC) No. USZ62-79221—Fredericksburg and Spotsylvania National Military Park, photographed by Charles Ledford (2); (NA) Neg. No. 111-B-3320. **47:** (LC) No. B-8184-10117—Eleanor S. Brockenbrough Library/The Museum of the Confederacy/Richmond, Va., photographed by Larry Sherer—MASS-MOLLUS/USAMHI, copied by A. Pierce Bounds. **48:** The Granger Collection, N.Y. **49:** The Moorland-Spingarn Research Center, Howard University, Washington, DC, copied by Larry Sherer. **50:** The Moorland-Spingarn Research Center, Howard University, photographed by Evan H. Sheppard—National Park Service, Frederick Douglass National Historic Site, photographed by J.H. Kent, Rochester, N.Y.; The Granger Collection, N.Y.—The Moorland-Spingarn Research Center, Howard University, Washington, DC, photographed by Larry Sherer. **51:** Courtesy Madison County Historical Society, Oneida, N.Y.—The Moorland-Spingarn Research Center, Howard University, Washington, DC—The Moorland-Spingarn Research Center, Howard University, photographed by Evan H. Sheppard (2)—Culver Pictures Inc. **52:** US Naval Historical Center Photograph. **53:** MASS-MOLLUS/USAMHI, copied by Robert Walch. **54:** US Naval Historical Center Photograph—The Huntington Library, San Marino, Calif.—The Museum of the Confederacy, Richmond, Va., photographed by Larry Sherer. **55:** J #1027 Manet, Edouard, "The Battle of the 'Kearsarge' and the 'Alabama,'" The John G. Johnson Collection, Philadelphia Museum of Art—Valentine Museum, Richmond, Va.—Victor R. Boswell, Jr., (c) National Geographic Society. **56:** The Western Reserve Historical Society, Cleveland, Ohio. **57:** The Museum of the Confederacy, Richmond, Va., photographed by Katherine Wetzel. **58:** Painting by W.H. Shelton, courtesy Gettysburg National Military Park, photographed by Larry Sherer—drawing by Alfred R. Waud, (LC); courtesy Bureau of State Office Buildings, Commonwealth of Massachusetts, photograph by Douglas Christian. **59:** North Carolina Division of Archives and History; from *MAPPING FOR STONEWALL: THE CIVIL WAR SERVICE OF JED HOTCHKISS* by William J. Miller, Elliott & Clark Publishing, Washington, DC, 1993; The Pejepscot Historical Society, Brunswick, Maine—The State Museum of Pennsylvania, Pennsylvania Historical and Museum Commission. **60:** (LC) No. BH834-78; painting by Thomas Nast, Private Collection—(LC) No. USZC4-977; inset, Manassas National Battlefield Park, photographed by Larry Sherer. **61:** (NA) Gift Collection Photo Number 200(s)-CC-2288, copied by Evan H. Sheppard—(LC). **62:** Lloyd Ostendorf Collection. **63:** National Museum of American History, Smithsonian Institution, Washington, DC, photographed by Dane Penland—NPS, Ford's Theatre Museum, Washington, DC, photographed by Edward Owen; The Abraham Lincoln Museum, Lincoln Memorial University, Harrogate, Tenn. **64, 65:** The Lincoln Museum, Fort Wayne, Ind.—Frank and Marie-Therese Wood Print Collections, Alexandria, Va.—National Postal Museum, Smithsonian Institution, Washington, DC—courtesy Christopher D.W. Nelson; (LC), photographed by Michael Latil(2); (LC), courtesy James R. Mellon—courtesy Harris Andrews; Frank and Marie-ThérèseWood Print Collections, Alexandria, Va. **66:** From *PHOTOGRAPHIC HISTORY OF THE CIVIL WAR: FORT SUMTER TO GETTYSBURG*, edited by William C. Davis and Bell I. Wiley, Black Dog & Leventhal Publishers, New York, 1994. **67:** The Museum of the Confederacy, photographed by Katherine Wetzel. **68:** (LC)—from *VIRGINIA MEDICAL MONTHLY*, vol. 88, Oct., 1961 p.595—courtesy of History of Medicine Division, National Library of Medicine (2); The Museum of the Confederacy, Richmond, Va., photographed by Katherine Wetzel. **69:** The Museum of the Confederacy, Richmond, Va., photographed by Katherine Wetzel (4)—(LC)—Phoebe Y. Pember Papers, Southern Historical Collection, Library of the University of North Carolina at Chapel Hill, photographed by Paul Dagys. **70:** The Bettmann Archive. **71:** The Brooklyn Historical Society on loan to the Museum of the Confederacy, Richmond, Va., photographed by Larry Sherer. **72:** The Archives of the University of Notre Dame, courtesy Sherman House; painting by George Peter Alexander Healy, National Museum of American Art, Washington, DC/Art Resource, N.Y.—The Archives of the University of Notre Dame (2)—Painting by Thure de Thulstrup, The Seventh Regiment Fund, Inc. **73:** (LC) No. B-8184-3626—The Kean Archives, Philadelphia, Pa.; National Postal Museum, Smithsonian Institution, Washington, DC. **74:** (NA) Neg. No. B-4914. **75:** Courtesy Cherokee National Historical Society, photographed by Don Wheeler. **76:** Courtesy Cherokee Studies Institute Inc., Gilmore Collection, photographed by Don Wheeler; General Sweeny's Museum, Republic, Mo.—courtesy Oklahoma Historical Society, No. 12699— Frank & Marie-Thérèse Wood Print Collections, Alexandria, Va.; inset, courtesy Cherokee Studies Institute Inc., Gilmore Collection, photographed by Don Wheeler. **77:** General Sweeny's Museum, Republic, Mo.—courtesy Oklahoma Historical Society, No. 1046.A—General Sweeny's Museum, Republic, Mo. **78:** (NA) Neg. No. 111-B-5889. **79:** The Navy Museum, Washington Navy Yard, Washington, D C, photographed by Evan H. Sheppard. **80, 81:** Painting by Willia Swain, National Portrait Gallery, Smithsonian Institution/Ar source, N.Y.; courtesy The Wadsworth Atheneum, Hartford, Citizens of Hartford by subscription May 24, 1886, photograp by Al Freni—The Historic New Orleans Collection, accessio 1974.80; courtesy The Atlanta History Center, photographed Bill Hull—The Navy Museum, Washington Navy Yard, Was ton, D C, photographed by Evan H. Sheppard. **82, 83:** Cour Mulberry Plantation, Camden, S.C., photographed by Alt Le **84:** Painting by Samuel Osgood, National Portrait Gallery, S sonian Institution/Art Resource, N.Y.; courtesy Mulberry Plar tion, Camden, S.C., photographed by Alt Lee, Inc.—Frank a Marie-Thérèse Wood Print Collections, Alexandria, Va. **85:** Library of Virginia; courtesy The South Caroliniana Library, University of South Carolina, photographed by Alt Lee, Inc.- courtesy Mulberry Plantation, Camden, S.C., photographed b Lee, Inc. **86:** (LC). **87:** Smithsonian Institution National N matic Collection, Washington, DC. **88, 89**: (LC) No. 29604 set, from *A PERSONAL HISTORY OF ULYSSES S. GRANT* Albert D. Richardson, American Publishing Co., Hartford, C 1868; courtesy The Civil War Library and Museum, Philadelp Pa., photographed by Andy Patilla; drawing by Alfred R. Wau (LC)—courtesy the Ohio Historical Society, OH5200; paintir Paul D. Philippotaux, Chicago Historical Society. **90:** Portrai Paul Louvrier, West Point Museum, US Military Academy, W Point, N.Y., photographed by Henry Groskinsky; inset, paintir George P.A. Healy, copyrighted by White House Historical A ation, photograph by National Geographic Society. **91:** Cour The Civil War Library and Museum, Philadelphia, Pa., photographed by Gib Ford—Frank and Marie-Thérèse Wood Prir Collections, Alexandria, Va; National Postal Museum, Smiths ian Institution, Washington, DC—from *THE END OF AN E VOLUME SIX OF THE IMAGE OF WAR 1861-1865*, Doub and Company, Inc., Garden City, N.Y., 1984; US Postal Servi **93:** Henry Groskinsky. **94, 95:** Laura Sikes.

ACKNOWLEDGMENTS

The editors wish to thank the following individuals and institution their valuable assistance in the preparation of this volume:

In the United States:

District of Columbia: Washington—John J. McDonough, Manuscri vision, Library of Congress; Harold Langley, Armed Forces History lections, Margaret Vining, National Museum of American History, Joseph Geraci, National Postal Museum, Smithsonian Institution; E ward M. Furgol, Charles Haberline, Naval Historical Center, Washi ton Navy Yard.

Georgia: Atlanta—Gordon Jones, Atlanta Historical Society.

Illinois: Chicago—Eileen Flanagan, Chicago Historical Society.

Indiana: Notre Dame—Charles Lamb, The Archives of the Univers Notre Dame.

Louisiana: New Orleans—Jude Solomon, The Historic New Orlean Collection.

Maryland: Frederick—Burton Kummerow, National Museum of Civ War Medicine. Glen Echo—Joseph E. Burns, Jr., Clara Barton Nati Historic Site.

Mississippi: Biloxi—Michael Wright, Beauvoir, The Jefferson Davis Shrine. Vicksburg—Terry Winshell, Vicksburg National Military Pa

Missouri: Republic—Thomas Sweeney.

New York: West Point—David Meschutt, West Point Museum, U.S. itary Academy.

North Carolina: Chapel Hill—Richard Shrader, John E. White, Sou Historical Collection, University of North Carolina.

Oklahoma: Oklahoma City—Chester Cowan, Oklahoma Historical ety. Tahlequah—Tom Mooney, Cherokee National Historical Societ Leon Gilmore.

Pennsylvania: Carlisle Barracks—Randy Hackenburg, Michael J. Wir United States Army Military History Institute. Gettysburg—Paul Shevchuk, Gettysburg National Military Park. Philadelphia—Steph Wright, Civil War Library and Museum; Caroline Demaree, Philade Museum of Art.

South Carolina: Camden—McCoy Hill; Martha Williams Daniels, M berry Plantation. Columbia—Beth Bilderbach, Allen H. Stokes, Sou Caroliniana Library, University of South Carolina.

Virginia: Alexandria—Frank and Marie Thérèse Wood. Annandale— Homer Babcock; Christopher D.W. Nelson. Fredericksburg—Janice Fredericksburg and Spotsylvania National Military Park. Lexington— Joanna Smith, Stonewall Jackson House, Historic Lexington Foundation; Julie Cline, News Office, Washington and Lee University. New News—John Pemberton, The Mariners' Museum. Richmond—Charl Cook; Petie Bogen-Garrett, The Library of Virginia; Jodi Koste, Tom kins-McCaw Library, Medical College of Virginia; Melinda Collier, M seum of the Confederacy; Teresa Roane, Valentine Museum; AnnMa Price, Virginia Historical Society. Winchester—Cissy Shull, Stonewa Jackson Headquarters Museum, Frederick County Historical Society.

West Virginia: Harpers Ferry—Linda Myers, Teresa Vasquez de Vado, tional Park Service, Harpers Ferry Center.

© 1995 UNITED STATES POSTAL SERVICE All rights reserved.

No part of this book may be reproduced in any form or by any electr or mechanical means, including information storage and retrieval devices or systems, without prior written permission from the publisher, cept that brief passages may be quoted for reviews.

First printing. Printed in U.S.A.

TIME-LIFE is a trademark of Time Warner Inc. U.S.A.

ISBN 0-8094-9191-5

THE STAMPS

[Monitor-Virginia] In an epic duel of ironclads, the USS *Monitor* and the CSS *Virginia* face off in Hampton Roads on March 9, 1862.

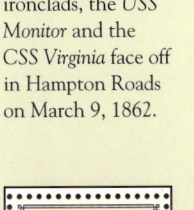

[Robert E. Lee] Ever firm and dignified in the face of adversity, Lee stands before his horse, Traveller, as the smoke of battle billows.

[Clara Barton] Seated in a Federal hospital tent, nurse Barton displays the mettle of one who saw the worst of the war and persevered.

[Ulysses Grant] Grant strikes the casual pose that belied his relentless desire to confront the enemy and win the war.

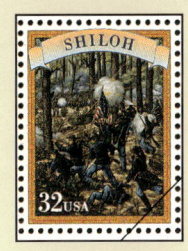

[Shiloh] Federals brave the sting of determined Confederates in the aptly named Hornet's Nest at Shiloh on April 6, 1862.

[Jefferson Davis] The Confederate President appears against a backdrop emblematic of the Old South he struggled to preserve.

[David Farragut] Farragut watches from the rigging of his flagship *Hartford* as his fleet advances on New Orleans in March 1862.

[Frederick Douglass] With hand raised to drive home his point, abolitionist Douglass exudes the conviction that roused audiences.

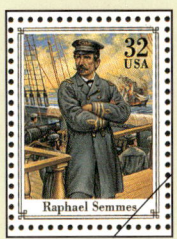

[Raphael Semmes] Semmes stands confidently aboard his commerce raider *Alabama* after claiming the Federal ship in the distance.

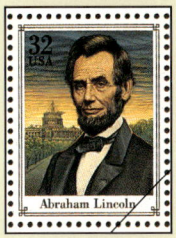

[Abraham Lincoln] The Union's vigilant commander in chief maintains his watch as dawn breaks over the unfinished Capitol.

[Harriet Tubman] Beckoning slaves to freedom, Tubman completes another daring journey on the Underground Railroad she helped maintain.

[Stand Watie] The hard-riding Cherokee commander gallops off in 1864 after raiding the Federal supply vessel in the background.

[Joseph E. Johnston] Johnston stands on Kennesaw Mountain, where his forces resisted Sherman's drive toward Atlanta in June 1864.

[Winfield Hancock] Resplendent astride his mount, Hancock prepares to lead his celebrated counterattack at Williamsburg in May 1862.

[Mary Chesnut] Diarist Chesnut adds an entry to the penetrating journal that chronicled hopes and fears on the Confederate home front.

[Chancellorsville] After flanking the foe on May 2, 1863, Jackson's men charge a Union battery to win the day at Chancellorsville.

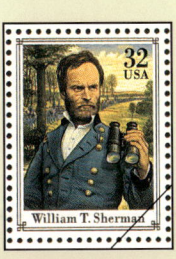

[William T. Sherman] Field glasses in hand Sherman leads a column of blue-clad soldiers in his relentless advance through the Deep South.

[Phoebe Pember] Confederate nurse Pember works to save a soldier in the wards, where infections could be as deadly as bullets.

["Stonewall" Jackson] Rigid in his comportment and dazzlingly quick in his tactical maneuvers, Jackson takes to the field astride Little Sorrel.

[Gettysburg] Federals on Cemetery Ridge beat back Pickett's charge on the last day at Gettysburg, July 3, 1863.

To receive your own souvenir edition, hardcover *Civil War* tabletop book featuring exciting stories, colorful illustrations and two full panes of these stamps, please call **1-800-STAMP24** or send $29.95 plus $4.20 for shipping and handling to:

Civil War Book Offer, U. S. Postal Service, Post Office Box 419219, Kansas City, MO 64141-6219

Please allow six weeks for delivery.

Offer expires July 1, 1996, or while supplies last. Offer valid only for orders delivered in the United States.

Shiloh
April 6-7, 1862

Confederates surprised Grant at Pittsburg Landing, TN, but lost General A. S. Johnston. Union counterattack at Shiloh Church forced Southerners to withdraw. Casualties: 13,050 Union, 10,700 Confederate.

**Union Lt. General
Ulysses S. Grant**
1822-1885

Gained national fame with "unconditional surrender" victory at Fort Donelson. Crafted brilliant wins at Vicksburg, Chattanooga. Forced Lee's surrender. U.S. President 1869-77.

**Union Nurse
Clara Harlowe Barton**
1821-1912

"Angel of the Battlefield" nursed the wounded at Antietam and at Virginia battlefields. Helped identify and mark graves at Andersonville prison. Founded American Red Cross.

**Confederate General
Robert Edward Lee**
1807-1870

Army of Northern Virginia Commander, 1862-65. Won Seven Days' Campaign, 2nd Manassas, Chancellorsville. Repelled at Gettysburg. Surrendered April 9, 1865. Became college president.

Monitor & Virginia (Merrimack)
March 9, 1862

In the first clash of the iron-clads, U.S.S. *Monitor* and C.S.S. *Virginia* battled to a stalemate, preserving U.S. blockade at Hampton Roads, VA. *Virginia* burned in May. Hatteras gale sank *Monitor*.

**16th U.S. President
Abraham Lincoln**
1809-1865

Illinois "Rail-Splitter" pursued war vigorously to restore the Union "of . . . by . . . for the people." Urged "malice toward none." Assassinated five days after Lee's surrender.

**Confederate Rear Admiral
Raphael Semmes**
1809-1877

Audacious commander of C.S.S. *Sumter* and *Alabama* plagued Union shipping, capturing or destroying more than 90 vessels. Professor, editor, lawyer. Wrote books of exploits.

**Journalist-Orator
Frederick Douglass**
1818-1895

"Wielding . . . pen . . . voice," ex-slave campaigned for rights for Blacks, women. Assisted runaways to Canada. Helped recruit Blacks for 54th Massachusetts Regiment. U.S. Minister to Haiti.

**Union Vice Admiral
David Glasgow Farragut**
1801-1870

A midshipman at age 9. Electrified the North with daring naval assault to capture New Orleans. Yelled "Damn the torpedoes! Full speed ahead!" during the attack at Mobile Bay.

**President of the Confederacy
Jefferson Finis Davis**
1808-1889

Ex-U.S.Senator from Mississippi, named provisional CSA head Feb.1861.Quarreled with military about war tactics and strategy but supported Lee. Captured May 1865 in GA, imprisoned two years.

**Confederate Diarist
Mary Boykin Miller Chesnut**
1823-1886

Astute, articulate hostess. Wife of aide to Jefferson Davis. Wrote of daily life, events, amid South's officialdom. Her plain-spoken journal, published posthumously, sparkles with wit and irony.

**Union Major General
Winfield Scott Hancock**
1824-1886

Brigade, Division, Corps Commander at Fredericks-burg, Chancellorsville. Played major role in Union victory at Gettysburg, but was severely wounded. Presidential candidate 1880.

**Confederate General
Joseph Eggleston Johnston**
1807-1891

Commander CSA forces Northern Virginia 1861-62. Wounded at Seven Pines. Master defensive strategist bickered often with Davis. Led Army of Tennessee, Dalton to Atlanta.

**Confederate Brig. General
Stand Watie (De-ga-do-ga)**
1806-1871

Known for guerrilla tactics tying down Union troops. Sole CSA Indian General raised Cherokee regiment, fought at Pea Ridge, captured federal steamboat. Last CSA General to surrender.

**Abolitionist
Harriet Ross Tubman**
c1821-1913

Fugitive slave who fled to freedom. As "Moses of her people," led over 200 Blacks north via Underground Railroad. Served Union Army as cook, spy and scout.

Gettysburg
July 1-3, 1863

Lee invaded North 2nd time. Encounter led to carnage as Union Gen. George Meade elected "to stay and fight," repelling Pickett's Charge. Casualties: 23,050 Union, 28,075 Confederate.

**Confederate Lt. General
Thomas Jonathan Jackson**
1824-1863

Nicknamed "Stonewall" at First Manassas. Brilliant tactician in Shenandoah Valley Campaign. Fatally wounded by own men after routing Union right flank at Chancellorsville.

**Confederate Nurse
Phoebe Yates Levy Pember**
1823-1913

Directed care and dietary needs of over 10,000 soldiers at Richmond's Chimborazo, one of CSA's largest hospitals. Specialty: chicken soup. Criticized poor care in her *A Southern Woman's Story*.

**Union Major General
William Tecumseh Sherman**
1820-1891

Blunt, grizzled strategist distinguished himself at Shi-loh and Vicksburg. Captured Atlanta. Introduced total warfare in his March across GA and through the Carolinas. Negotiated lenient peace.

Chancellorsville
May 1-4, 1863

Greatly outnumbered, Lee boldly split forces, routed Hooker's Union army. Mortal wounding of Stonewall Jackson overshadowed Rebel victory. Casualties: 17,300 Union, 12,800 Confederate.

(Affix stamps and mount here)

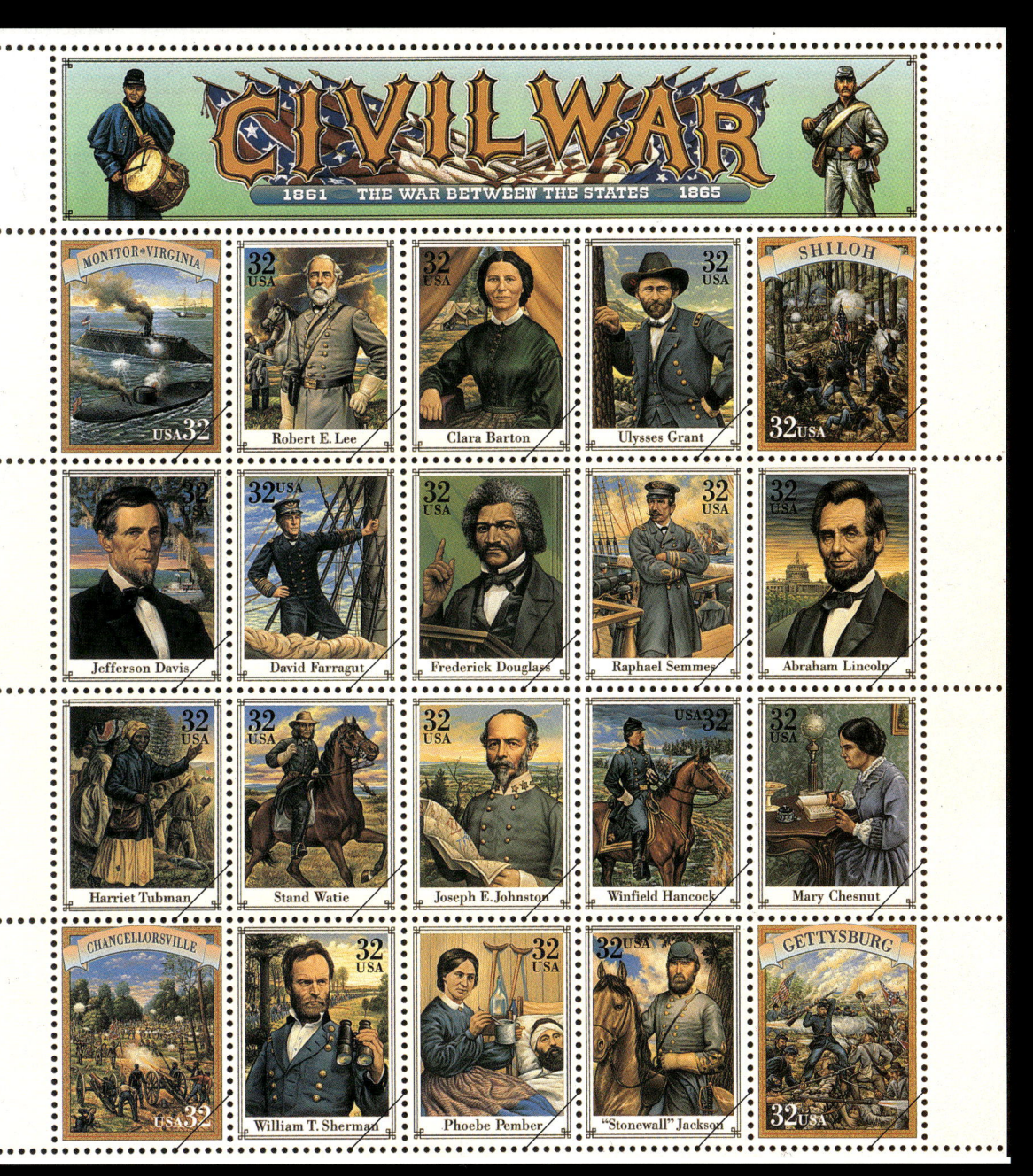

(Affix stamps and mount here)